INTENTIONAL
DISCIPLEMAKING

CULTIVATING SPIRITUAL MATURITY
IN THE LOCAL CHURCH

Ron Bennett

NAVPRESS

Bringing Truth to Life
P.O. Box 35001, Colorado Springs, Colorado 80935

OUR GUARANTEE TO YOU

The Navigators is an international Christian organization. Our mission is to reach, disciple, and equip people to know Christ and to make Him known through successive generations. We envision multitudes of diverse people in the United States and every other nation who have a passionate love for Christ, live a lifestyle of sharing Christ's love, and multiply spiritual laborers among those without Christ.

NavPress is the publishing ministry of The Navigators. NavPress publications help believers learn biblical truth and apply what they learn to their lives and ministries. Our mission is to stimulate spiritual formation among our readers.

© 2001 by Ron Bennett
All rights reserved. No part of this publication may be reproduced in any form without written permission from NavPress, P.O. Box 35001, Colorado Springs, CO 80935.
www.navpress.com
Library of Congress Catalog Card Number: 2001030857
ISBN 1-57683-262-7

Cover design by Dan Jamison
Cover illustration by Nip Rogers / Images.com
Creative Team: Pam Mellskog, Amy Spencer, Pat Miller

Some of the anecdotal illustrations in this book are true to life and are included with the permission of the persons involved. All other illustrations are composites of real situations, and any resemblance to people living or dead is coincidental.

Unless otherwise identified, all Scripture quotations in this publication are taken from *The HOLY BIBLE: NEW INTERNATIONAL VERSION*® (NIV®). Copyright © 1973, 1978, 1984 by International Bible Society. Used by permission of Zondervan Publishing House. All rights reserved. Other versions used include the *New American Standard Bible* (NASB), © The Lockman Foundation 1960, 1962, 1963, 1968, 1971, 1972, 1973, 1975, 1977, 1995; and *The Message: New Testament with Psalms and Proverbs* by Eugene H. Peterson, copyright © 1993, 1994, 1995, used by permission of NavPress Publishing Group.

Bennett, Ron.
    Intentional disciplemaking : cultivating spiritual maturity in the local church / Ron Bennett.
        p. cm.
    Includes bibliographical references.
    ISBN 1-57683-262-7
    1. Discipling (Christianity) I. Title.

BV4520 .B39 2001
253—dc21   2001030857

Printed in the United States of America

1 2 3 4 5 6 7 8 9 10 / 05 04 03 02 01

To Dad
for his infectious spirit of adventure

To Mom
for her persistent protection of prayer

10/6/43

Contents

Preface

WHY ANOTHER BOOK on discipleship? After all, isn't every church making disciples? Won't people mature if you just offer authentic fellowship, creative worship, and solid preaching? With plenty of programs already crowding the church calendar, who has time to get more involved? Church leaders can hardly get members to serve the way it is. On top of everything else, many churches are growing and handling the crowds by offering two services or launching a building campaign.

Typically, church growth involves more people, bigger facilities, expanding budgets, larger staff, and a greater multiplicity of programs. But this book isn't about church growth; it's about depth—spiritual maturity through intentional disciplemaking leaders and communities. To assess the need for this type of focus—even within the busiest ministries—consider these wake-up-call questions:

What impact does your ministry have on the culture in which it exists? How much does it shape the morals, character, agenda, perceptions, and worldview of those in the local community? Are you acting, or being acted upon?

How effective is your ministry in populating heaven and depopulating hell? Is the kingdom of God being added to or simply rearranged as members church-hop? Are authentic disciples being made of those who convert to Christianity?

Are the lives of believers radically changed as a result of their encounter with your ministry? Does transformation take place, or do members simply conform to a religious set of norms? Is Christlikeness actually being manifested through the lives of individual believers in private and in community?

This book focuses on changing the way you view the discipleship process. Disciples are made, not born. In other words, unlike weeds, disciples don't just happen. Rather, they sprout and bloom into full maturity when Christian individuals and communities focus on developing spiritual maturity the way Jesus intended—by closely following Him in every part of life.

Para-church ministries typically succeed in creating intentional disciplemaking communities on campuses or military bases. There, many men and women are launched into the discipleship process. However, when as alumni they move to other communities and churches, they often find a disconnect between what they have experienced and what the church at large models.

Disciplemaking never occurs in isolation (it ranges from one-on-one mentoring to corporate outreach), so how can a ministry cultivate an environment where spiritual maturity is expected and the fruit of that maturity influences the dominant culture? Much has been written about what it takes to do this. My intent is not to repeat that information. Rather, ministry leaders can use this book for fresh ideas on how to make disciples who know how to make disciples— those passionate about this Christian mission.

Your ministry may be with youth, Xers, Boomers, or a combination thereof. It may be with small groups or adult education. You may be a pastor, an elder, or a leader of a specialized ministry. You may be the initiator of a home-based church or marketplace ministry. Whatever the case, if you have a vision and heart for developing multiple spiritual generations of fruitful disciples, this book is for you!

Acknowledgments

M Y BEST FRIEND and wife, Mary, has been a constant source of encouragement and support in the adventure of preparing this material. She has been my ministry partner and greatest fan. Without her support, I would never have attempted to put these ideas into print. Her listening ear and quiet wisdom have contributed more than she will ever know.

Bob Walz, along with other Navigator staff, has been a source of insight and challenge. Bob especially has been a sounding board and a refiner of ideas. His constant challenge was to say it better.

CHAPTER ONE

Arrested Spiritual Development?

In fact, though by this time you ought to be teachers, you need someone to teach you the elementary truths of God's word all over again. You need milk, not solid food!

Hebrews 5:12

G ROWING UP IS so common and predictable it's taken for granted. Until May 1975, when our first child was born, my wife, Mary, and I thought we could just stand back and watch it happen. We had been eagerly planning and anticipating the miracle as only first-time parents can. We had prepared the room, taken the prenatal classes, and saved for the down payment. The work was done, and we were ready!

Our anticipation heightened when Mary went into labor. Driving to the hospital, we looked forward to getting through the birthing event so we could begin the exciting process of rearing a family. We had spent hours talking about what it would be like to have a baby that grew to be a toddler, then a child, then a young adult, then a father or mother. We reminisced about our own childhoods—what parts were difficult and what parts were enjoyable. And we critiqued the parenting practices of our folks, eventually deciding what to use and what to discard.

Many hours after arriving at the hospital that morning, Bryan came into our world and opened this long-awaited new chapter of discovery and growth. However, we had barely laid eyes on him when nurses swaddled our baby boy and whisked him to another room for observation. Mary used the time apart to enjoy a well-deserved rest, and I fell into bed at home, exhausted from Lamaze breathing cycles.

When the phone rang, I thought that I must have been asleep for a day and had missed going back to the hospital to visit the family. First, I picked up the alarm clock. Before setting it down and grabbing the phone, I noticed with relief that only an hour had passed since I had returned home and hit the pillow.

Mary spoke on the other end of the line, but soon she faltered in sharing the grave news and began to cry. That's when the pediatrician gently took the receiver from her hand to explain. "Bryan is having some difficulty breathing," the doctor began. "We have checked his heart and lungs, and they are okay. We think it's his brain."

The twenty-minute trip back to the hospital seemed like an eternity as I created and recreated every conceivable scenario to figure out what could have gone wrong. Eventually, I reasoned that whatever was happening could only be temporary, given the power of modern medicine. To steady my nerves, I reminded myself that Mary was fine, that this crisis only represented a blip on the screen. We would get through it.

As soon as I reached Mary's room, the hospital staff brought Bryan to us. The wires, monitors, IVs, and attendants around him created quite a spectacle—but not for long. The doctor ducked in to apprise us of Bryan's condition, and he advised transporting him immediately to a neonatal intensive care unit sixty miles away. We hastily signed the necessary forms and watched hospital staffers hurry from the room, leaving us alone in the deafening silence of our ache, fear, and tears.

Bryan is now twenty-five years old. Although he has logged about three hundred months—9,125 days—on Earth, he has never walked, never seen the sun, and never said

INTENTIONAL DISCIPLEMAKING

"Dad" or "Mom," he has never played baseball, run through a sprinkler, or given us a hug. Immediately after his birth, Bryan became a prisoner in his own body when severe brain damage created multiple handicaps that permanently jammed his maturation process. Consequently, he has had twenty-five years of living, but only nine months of normal, healthy development.

As his parents, we love him deeply—as much as we love our other three children. Yet his inability to mature has robbed him and us of God's design for life. We have learned to accept Bryan just as he is, to relate to him at his level of understanding. Because he can't see, we simply touch. Because he can't speak, we talk. Because he can't reach out to us, we hug him. Still, we occasionally wonder what life would be like had Bryan grown up.

God must feel a similar sadness and pain when His children get "stuck" at spiritual infancy, childhood, or adolescence—when they never reach spiritual adulthood with all the privileges and responsibilities it entails. Of course, God's love remains constant and immeasurable regardless. But like a human parent, God can also feel disappointment, pain, and loss.

Certainly, some Christians remain in this kind of disappointing spiritual infancy because, for one reason or another, they do not want to grow up. However, plenty of folks get "stuck" because church leaders lack the knowledge, skills, and resources to develop healthy, maturing followers of Christ. That's the bad news. The good news is that church leaders can become more deliberate about making disciples—mature Christians who practice their faith, share it, and reproduce it in others.

Consider your church. Are the leaders committed to creating an environment that supports healthy spiritual growth for a lifetime? Are people being trained and empowered to be effective spiritual fathers and mothers? Is immaturity a result of information without opportunities to apply it to their lives? Do you expect key events alone to create maturity in each member?

During Christ's time, "disciple" was a common term that described someone who adhered to the teachings of another. The core meaning revolved around learning, and for centuries it was in vogue to be known as a follower of someone. Hence, disciples followed Moses, Socrates, Plato, and even the Pharisees. But Jesus took this common term and redefined it. He gave it a new meaning. To Christ, discipleship was following Him, not just His principles, ideas, or philosophy. It was not primarily conceptual but personal. It was not a vague ideal but a concrete relationship that had definition. For instance, He would end instructive statements by saying, "Without this, you cannot be my disciple."

An overview of the Gospels reveals that Jesus specifically gave points of reference as to what makes someone His disciple: commitment, competence, character, and conviction. While not comprehensive, the following describes what Jesus expected when He commanded the apostles to "make disciples."

Commitment

Large crowds were traveling with Jesus, and turning to them He said:

> "If anyone comes to me and does not hate his father and mother, his wife and children, his brothers and sisters—yes, even his own life—he cannot be my disciple. And anyone who does not carry his cross and follow me cannot be my disciple."
> (Luke 14:26-27; see also Luke 9:23-24)

In Christ's day, it was enough to adhere to a teacher's instruction. It was a teacher/pupil relationship, after all. However, disciples of the Messiah needed to be committed to the *person* of Jesus—not to a cause, a church, an ideal, or even a set of truths. For with Jesus, everything hung on who He was and is. His teaching flowed out of His person. Believe it or not, you can follow the teachings of Christ and never really recognize who He is (as distinct from God and the Holy Spirit), much less commit to imitating Him.

There are many areas in the family of God that allow for blending and being interdependent, but discipleship is not one of them. We can learn in groups, we can serve in teams, we can worship as a family, but we can only be disciples individually. A ministry that seeks to make disciples must support the personal responsibility and accountability required in developing individual discipleship. It can use a variety of methods, but it must always bring discipleship to the personal level of each individual.

It was this principle that both attracted and threatened me in my early journey with Christ. I was pleased to discover that Christ personally called me to follow Him. I was significant, valuable, and important to Him. I wasn't just a faceless name in a sea of humanity. At the university, I was a number in a computer. With Christ, I was a unique individual.

I appreciated that God sees each person as an Abraham, as the beginning of many generations. In the midst of chaos and confusion, God still seeks for an individual man or woman to make up the wall and stand before Him on behalf of the land (see Ezekiel 22:30).

As I became more serious about my faith, I realized that Christ's personal challenge to follow Him caused me to squirm. There was no one to hide behind. He asked me to deny myself, take up my cross, and follow. There was no team effort here—just Jesus and me.

I knew my journey with Christ depended on whether I was willing to let go and reach up to put my hand in His. Each time I took another step of commitment and surrender, I realized the truth of His promise, "Come to me . . . and I will give you rest. . . . My burden is light" (Matthew 11:28,30).

Any ministry that is intentional about discipleship will encourage this type of commitment to grow as an apprentice of Jesus. Why? Because commitment is basic to knowing Christ and seeking His kingdom first. Without commitment, discipleship can't happen.

Competence

"If you remain in me and my words remain in you, ask whatever you wish, and it will be given you. This is to my Father's glory, that you bear much fruit, showing yourselves to be my disciples." (John 15:7-8)

One young woman had been consumed for several years with mothering her two preschool children. Because she stayed at home so much, she felt anxious when invited to go out for dinner with her husband and the board of directors from the company of his employ. She worried that her vocabulary had shrunk to monosyllabic words only, and she wondered if she could converse about anything other than Dr. Seuss or Sesame Street. Nonetheless, the evening seemed to unfold without a hitch.

She hazarded her husband's opinion during the drive home: Had she sounded like an adult? Had she embarrassed herself or him? He reassured her that she had, indeed, sounded knowledgeable on a variety of topics and had used "big" words. With a sigh, she leaned back in her seat until he added his final comment: "Next time, though, please let me cut my own meat!"

Spiritually speaking, everybody needs his or her own knife and fork. Paul reminds Timothy to be a diligent "workman who does not need to be ashamed and who correctly handles the word of truth" (2 Timothy 2:15). Very often, however, spiritual competence never develops. For instance, I recently visited a couple that had just changed churches—again—due to a form of spiritual immaturity. "We were not getting fed," they complained. Certainly church leadership must feed its flock, but sometimes leaders unwittingly keep people dependent on processed food instead of helping them learn how to process their own. Immature Christians always rely on someone else to expound the Word.

Hence, effective discipleship involves teaching self-feeding skills—competence in studying the Bible and in applying it to daily living. The disciplemaking community's motto should be, "Knives and forks for everyone!"

In the mid-1980s, I served as one of eight elders in a church wrestling with its biblical position on a certain issue. After the pastor introduced the issue, he asked each elder to study the Bible for insight. We agreed to study and return the next month prepared to discuss the topic and pound out the church's official position.

When we reassembled, the pastor revisited the issue and asked for discussion. He met silence! Only he and I had done any personal study. One elder even turned to me and whispered, "I don't know why he is making such a big deal out of this. Why doesn't he just tell us what the answer is so we can get on with the rest of the agenda?" This man never put his hands on his knife and fork. In fact, he had no interest in using them, much less in becoming competent.

Character

"A new command I give you: Love one another. As I have loved you, so you must love one another. By this all men will know that you are my disciples, if you love one another." (John 13:34-35)

Love is the most telling hallmark of an authentic Christian disciple. Of course, knowledge and service stem from the growth process, too. But without love, your credibility both inside and outside of the family of God dwindles. Love is so key to Christian maturity that the Bible says nonChristians can assess you based on its evidence. But to love the way Christ loves takes spiritual depth; it takes Christlike character.

In *Celebration of Discipline*, Richard Foster writes,

Superficiality is the curse of our age. The doctrine of instant satisfaction is a primary spiritual problem. The desperate need today is not for a greater number of intelligent people, or gifted people, but for deep people. The classical disciplines of the spiritual life call us to move beyond surface living into the depths.[1]

However, if we fail to place character-developing spiritual disciplines in a context of grace, they can get distorted into legalistic discouragements. Furthermore, while character development through various disciplines encourages spiritual maturity, everyone must understand that leading a more disciplined, spiritually mature life cannot make anyone more or less acceptable to God.

Rather, the discipleship growth process involves a marvelous mix of human discipline and God's grace. Remember the apostle Paul's emphasis on putting off the old man and putting on the new? Transformation and maturity result not only from the discipline of the individual, but also from the work of God's Spirit. For instance, the "God is at work in you" concept in Philippians 2:13 focuses on divine influence. On the other hand, the idea of working out your own salvation, as mentioned in the preceding verse (2:12), focuses on the *ways*, or disciplines, we pursue to work it out.

Foster categorizes spiritual disciplines as

- inward (meditation, prayer, fasting, study),
- outward (simplicity, solitude, submission, service), and
- corporate (confession, worship, guidance, celebration).

When I got involved with The Navigators ministry as a college student more than thirty years ago, I was discipled around the spiritual disciplines of Bible study, prayer, fellowship, and witnessing. Each approach supports character development, so long as it promotes Christlikeness.

Conviction

"You shall know the truth and the truth shall set you free" still sprawls over the heavy, giant doors of the Gothic library at my alma mater, Iowa State University in Ames (see John 8:32). But I never believed that knowing what was in that library would lead to freedom. Rather, I understood that verse in its original Christian context—that understanding God's truth and realizing His authority lead to freedom.

It is not the *knowing* but the *holding* of truth that marks someone as a disciple of Christ. Too often, Christians are knowledge rich, but application poor. We pride ourselves in having "right" doctrine, but without conviction—the kind that leads to commitment, competence, and character development—our lifestyles differ little from the cultural norm and don't even hint at Christ within us.

It is not surprising that both Paul and Peter had an image of spiritual maturity in mind as they carried out their ministries. They knew what it looked like and had a plan to encourage the critical process that produced it.

For instance, during his ministry Paul wrote to churches operating at different stages of collective maturity, dealing with a variety of problems over a number of years. Despite the churches' differing circumstances, a discipleship pattern emerged in his letters. He placed Christ at the foundation of the community, and then he added three levels consisting of faith, hope, and love. He either commended the individual church for following this building plan or exhorted the church for not following the plan. These four themes—Christ, faith, hope, and love—are interrelated and essential for spiritual maturity, and Paul drove them home at every opportunity.

"How can you recognize maturity in a church?" asks Gene Getz in *Sharpening the Focus of the Church*. "Maturity in the body of Christ can be identified by the enduring virtues. The degree of completeness can be measured by the degree to which the church manifests faith, hope and love."[2]

Peter also wrote to believers scattered throughout the Roman world to remind them that spiritual maturity involves acquiring a divine nature: qualities that stem from Christ's character. Peter encouraged believers to "make every effort" to grow in this way:

> Add to your faith goodness; and to goodness, knowledge; and to knowledge, self-control; and to self-control, perseverance; and to perseverance, godliness; and to godliness, brotherly kindness; and to brotherly kindness, love. For if you possess these qualities in increasing measure, they will keep you from being ineffective and unproductive in your knowledge of our Lord Jesus Christ. (2 Peter 1:5-8)

In addition to identifying the qualities of spiritual maturity, Peter recognized the process of building one virtue on top of another. Both Peter and Paul understood that spiritual maturity comes not simply from a design, but from great effort. It begins with personal effort and can be encouraged in a disciplemaking community.

At The Chapel in Akron, Ohio, Senior Pastor Knute Larson's concern about the need for adult fellowship prompted him to develop Adult Bible Fellowships (ABFs) and to write *The ABF Book* (The Chapel Press, 1991). ABFs organize Sunday school classes around more-focused Bible study and fellowship. Today, twenty years later, the three pilot ABFs have grown to as many as fifty. That's fifty groups of people discovering the beauty of group Bible study and fellowship. But are those people becoming disciples?

The Chapel's leadership tried answering that question with conviction by exploring the biblical concept of individual discipleship. This team underwent a two-year process of identifying what kind of person the church should be trying to develop. The process started at a pastoral retreat in the fall of 1996 as they attempted to answer how the Bible characterizes a mature Christian believer and what The Chapel's role should be in facilitating that process.

Ultimately, the leaders—under their pastor of discipleship, Jay Halley—outlined seven characteristics that now form the core of The Chapel's disciplemaking environment: learner, reproducer, server, relater, worshiper, rester, and giver. The church uses the manifestation of these characteristics in the lives of its members to determine its success in developing spiritually mature believers.

To stay sharp, the leader of each church program periodically evaluates how that program contributes to the seven characteristics of a disciple. The church also asks each person to candidly assess his or her spiritual journey so it can continue to enhance the growth process in these seven areas—and to prevent the tragedy of arrested development.

CHAPTER TWO

Discipleship
Blueprints

For every house is built by someone, but God is the
builder of everything.

Hebrews 3:4

A T THE EASTBOURNE Consultation on Discipleship
in the fall of 1999, leaders from more than fifty-four
countries representing nearly ninety organizations, denomi-
nations, and churches presented the following statement
regarding the definition of discipleship:

> While there are valid differences of perspective on
> what constitutes discipleship, we define Christian
> discipleship as a process that takes place within
> accountable relationships over a period of time for
> the purpose of bringing believers to spiritual matu-
> rity in Christ. Biblical examples suggest that disci-
> pleship is both relational and *intentional*, both
> position and process. . . . We will pursue the
> process of discipleship, just as *purposefully* as the
> proclamation of the Gospel. Evangelism and disci-
> pleship must be seen as integral [emphasis added].[1]

Without a clear disciplemaking purpose and strategy, various ministry programs—no matter how well intentioned the design—prove ineffective. Why? Because the programs keep people occupied but not developed enough to experience the rewards and responsibilities spiritual maturity brings. Furthermore, without substantive equipping, individuals can more easily slip from those programs back into the passive fringe of the Christian community.

With good reason, Christ's command to "make disciples" represents the purpose of ministry, not an afterthought. And discipleship doesn't happen by sitting in a spiritual greenhouse, but by design, effort, and perseverance on an individual level.

Imagine a businessperson coming to a town to establish a new venture. He buys land and builds offices, warehouses, and production facilities. He impresses the townspeople with his industry, and they become curious.

After months of preparation, when the facilities near completion, a long-awaited "help wanted" ad appears in the local newspaper. Word spreads quickly that this business offers excellent pay and benefits, and needs all skills. The already low unemployment rate plunges to zero as anyone who applies gets hired. You even quit your job to hire on.

When the business opens its doors, all the employees eagerly show up for work. At first, they stand in awe of the wealth of resources amassed in this facility. The warehouse is full of the latest machinery and technology as well as plenty of building materials. Eventually, however, a question begins to sweep over the huge crowd of idle workers. It begins as a whisper and gets louder: "What are we supposed to produce?" No one knows. They forgot to ask, and upper management never announced it.

Finally, you volunteer to approach the owner. A polite, well-dressed secretary ushers you into the owner's downtown office, and you find him sitting calmly at his glossy wood-paneled desk. "How are things going over at the plant?" the owner nonchalantly asks, glancing over the top of his bifocals while leafing through a stack of papers.

"Fine," you reply with your hat in hand. "We are all impressed with what you have built. We can't believe the high-tech equipment that you set up, and we are eager to get to work. But we do have one question. . . . What are we supposed to produce?"

"Produce?" responds the CEO incredulously. "Produce? Why, what difference does it make? Just get busy and produce something!"

Believe it or not, too often some do church that way, but they don't even stop to ask the question. They just get busy doing something—anything—and treat God as though He doesn't care or has no particular plan about what to develop with His resources.

The New Testament also uses the building metaphor to describe the process of discipleship. In 1 Corinthians 3:10, Paul refers to himself as "a wise master builder"(NASB) and warns others contributing to the building process to use the proper materials. Peter encourages building our spiritual house with Christ as the cornerstone.

Any ministry serious about making disciples is like a spiritual construction company. Its mission involves building solid communities by building sound homes—not entertainment centers, hospitals, theological universities, warehouses, shopping malls, community centers, or political action organizations. These homes represent the transformation of individual lives.

Disciplemaking ministries—or ongoing building projects—would do well to hang a permanent sign over the doors that reads, "Under Construction: Hardhat Area!" Sometimes construction requires destruction—building up as well as tearing down. Regardless, in a building zone we should always expect to see partially finished homes. We should also see someone on the premises making sure that these homes get completed according to the blueprint.

For fifteen years, Mary and I had lived in houses someone else planned and built. However, our move to Kansas City gave us the opportunity to build our own home. We purchased land, found a builder, and launched into our adventure.

Herb, our general contractor and mentor, walked us through the building process. Although the process was new to us, it was routine to Herb. He had "been there, done that." He was a professional who knew what needed to be done and who could do it.

The first question Herb asked us was, "What do you want your home to look like?" He didn't assume that we were going to hire him to build his dream home with our money. We had looked at model homes and design books. We had ideas and possibilities. We had a budget and a banker. But what we really needed was an actual blueprint.

Herb couldn't build without it, so he initially focused on turning our ideas into a set of working blueprints. Everyone who played a role in the building process was given a copy of those blueprints. Ours were not elaborate and, by some standards, not even detailed. But every subcontractor had to follow them. Some requested close examination of the plans, while others needed only general concepts. Whatever the case, the blueprints kept us all working together to make the dream house a reality.

That set of blueprints—now faded, wrinkled, and dirty—was the one thing that held all the different people together to achieve this goal. It was our guide, arbitrator, and judge, and we used it many times to resolve misunderstandings and conflicts.

Unfortunately, what seems like common sense in the physical world too often becomes the exception in the spiritual world. Discipleship efforts often flounder not due to a lack of spiritual terms or religious ideas, but because leaders don't create and communicate an easily understood blueprint.

When I discuss discipleship with church leaders struggling in that area, I typically return to the question Herb asked us: "What do you want your house to look like?" Then I probe deeper: "If a person gets involved in a disciplemaking ministry, what kind of change do you anticipate seeing in that person in the next five years? Could you explain the effects of long-term discipleship to new members if they asked?" If, as the leader, you lack a blueprint and vision of what the transformation will look like, how can you expect others to know—much less contribute to—the process?

A good disciplemaking blueprint may be detailed or fairly simple, but it must be biblical. It must reflect God's design, even though we may draft versions of that master plan in a variety of ways. It must ultimately result in disciples (fruitful followers of Christ, fully devoted followers of Christ, mature believers, and so on).

Besides the building metaphor, the New Testament also pictures disciplemaking as cultivating a field, running a race, and rearing a family. Although these scenarios reveal different perspectives on maturity, the notion of process runs through each as a common thread. Here's a closer look at the process of successfully discipling a childish Christian into a mature adult through the family model.

Childhood

Every believer needs a foundational understanding of what it means to be a child of God and the security implicit in this human/divine relationship. New Testament writers use the images of both birth and adoption to underscore the significant initial change that takes place when a person accepts Christ as Savior.

In 1 John 2:12-13, the apostle used two different words in Greek for "child." The first, *teknia*, is a general term for believers in God's family and emphasizes the relationship of child to father. John also used *paidia* for "child," which highlights the dependence of children on their parents. God delights in this dependence, because it characterizes a true spiritual child. Recognizing this dependence is the first stage of maturity.

Adulthood

In medieval Europe, a page progressed to squire and then to knight. Native Americans hold ceremonies that signal the passage of a boy to a man. In the majority of our society, there is no clear line of demarcation between adolescence and adulthood. Nonetheless, we still recognize that adulthood should occur somewhere around the late teens or early twenties. At that point, physical growth makes children look like adults. But only inner maturity makes them act like adults.

The apostle John refers to those who've matured past childhood as "young men" (1 John 2:13-14). At this stage, men and women know how to put on the full armor of God and to stand and fight in victory. John says the Word dwells in them: they know the Word and how to use it. They are no longer children in their thinking (see 1 Corinthians 14:20).

Parenthood

John continues to expand the picture of maturity from childhood to adulthood to parenthood (see 1 John 2:13-14). Who are the spiritual mothers and fathers? Spiritual parents are Christians who have a history of experiencing the reality of Christ and are now mature and responsible enough to encourage spiritual growth in others.

Developing a spiritual heritage stands out as a key scriptural theme. In John 17, Jesus prayed not just for His current disciples, but also for those who would believe through them. Moses exhorted fathers to teach their children, which ultimately could influence three generations. Paul encouraged Timothy to invest in faithful men who could reach others. In each of these example, at least three generations were affected. Intentional disciplemaking communities need to create this same expectation: spiritual parenting involves developing a third generation.

In general, the third generation gets attention. Just watch grandparents. They carry wallet-sized photos not of their children, but of their grandchildren. They beam with pride and lavish praise on the third generation. It's as if some unwritten law says you shouldn't brag on your own kids, but don't hold back on the grandkids.

Spiritual generations are God's strategy for reaching the world. Any plan that ignores the natural process of parenting through successive generations is doomed to fail because it circumvents God's design for maturity. Furthermore, failure to pass on the truths of the faith to another generation is a mark of immaturity in the church.

The writer of Hebrews felt uncomfortable with the immaturity of his audience. He knew that enough time had passed for them to be spiritual parents, that they should be teaching others. Therefore, he rebuked them for needing to return to elementary instruction when they should have been moving on to a more advanced growth phase of discipleship.

In some cases, an underdeveloped sense of stewardship stifles spiritual growth. Remember that a steward is someone entrusted to manage another's affairs, finances, or possessions. Jesus said,

"Whoever can be trusted with very little can also be trusted with much, and whoever is dishonest with very little will also be dishonest with much. So if you have not been trustworthy in handling worldly wealth, who will trust you with true riches? And if you have not been trustworthy with someone else's property, who will give you property of your own?" (Luke 16:10-12)

Abraham stands out as a model of faithful stewardship because he agreed to sacrifice his son on a mountain in Moriah to obey God. Thankfully, Abraham was spiritually mature enough to relinquish his ownership in favor of stewardship. No wonder, then, that God chose Abraham to father many descendants—both physically and spiritually.

Caring for children in the family of God is a critical aspect of stewardship. Reflecting on his ministry with the Thessalonians, Paul identifies his role as that of a mother who tenderly cares for and faithfully exhorts her children (see 1 Thessalonians 2:7-8). And Jesus gave His disciples a challenging picture of the sacrifice and stewardship required to disciple, or parent, immature Christians:

"Listen carefully: Unless a grain of wheat is buried in the ground, dead to the world, it is never any more than a grain of wheat. But if it is buried, it sprouts and reproduces itself many times over."
(John 12:24, *The Message*)

When I was growing up, my dad seemed to be constantly working on cars. He had been a mechanic earlier in his life and loved to repair old cars that we acquired as our family vehicles. If we came home from school and saw a car in the driveway with fenders on it, we knew we had a visitor. Having grown accustomed to riding in cars in various stages of repair or disrepair, we were thrilled one day to find out that an uncle had loaned us his new Chrysler for a few months while he was away on business. Not only was it a whole car, it was also a new one!

Being a steward of my uncle's car had some interesting effects on our family. For instance, we didn't get too attached because we knew we had to eventually return it. In fact, we probably took better care of the car without the title in hand. After all, we knew that there would be a day of reckoning for the condition of the car, that we would be held accountable for any damages.

"Keep your feet off the seats!" was the standard parental greeting whenever we got into my uncle's car. It was so predictable that we would all say it in unison as a prerequisite for entry. But more than fearing his wrath, my family wanted him to be pleased when he returned. We wanted him to feel he had made a wise decision entrusting his new car to us.

The parable Jesus taught about the wise and foolish stewards illustrates that people are responsible not only for protecting their talents, but also for investing them (see Matthew 25:14-30). Discovering how God has designed and gifted you is part of learning to be a faithful steward. An intentional disciplemaking community will provide the opportunity for maturing adults to discover and utilize their strengths and gifts.

The following chart provides indicators that can serve as

Spiritual Maturity Profile

Trait/Indicator	Child	Adult	Parent
COMMITMENT	To God's Word as truth (2 Timothy 3:16)	Christ as leader of life (Matthew 4:19)	Discipling others (Matthew 28:19-20)
	To God's family; identify with (Hebrews 10:24-25)	Serving others (Philippians 2:3-4)	Kingdom vision; God's heart for people every-where (John 3:16; 2 Peter 3:9)
COMPETENCE	Fellowship with God through the Word and prayer and with others in God's family (1 John 1:1-3)	Feed themselves on God's Word; abiding in Christ (John 8:31-32; Hebrews 5:12)	Follow up of new believers (Hebrews 5:12)
	Share personal faith story with others (Acts 1:8)	Share the gospel with lost people, guiding them to personal faith in Christ (Romans 1:16)	Use of their gifts effectively (1 Corinthians 12:12-13)
CHARACTER	Sensitivity toward sin—an honesty with God and others (1 John 1:9)	Love for others, other focus; servant spirit (John 13:34-35)	Self-sacrificing (1 Thessalonians 2:8-9)
	Love for Christ (John 14:21)	Self control— exercising spiri-tual and personal disciplines (1 Timothy 4:7-8)	Godliness (1 Timothy 6:11, 4:12)
CONVICTION	Identify with Christ; loved, valuable in Christ (2 Corinthians 5:17)	Living by faith and in the power of His Spirit (Hebrews 11:6)	Worth of every individual (Romans 12:3-4)
	Authority and reliability of the Word (1 Peter 2:2; Hebrews 4:12)	Character of God; confident in His promises (2 Peter 1:3-4)	Value of spiritual generations; spiritual heritage (3 John 4; 2 Timothy 2.2)

a starting point to evaluate how focused your church leadership is on developing spiritual parents.

With this biblical profile of spiritual maturity in mind, consider these assessment questions to begin building your new blueprint for disciplemaking:

- How far along are your leaders in the maturity process?
- Do you have spiritual children, adults, and parents in the church, or are most remaining in the child stage?
- Do you have people parenting who lack the foundation and training of a spiritually mature person?

Other critical questions address the activities that gobble ministry resources. Do those activities provide the necessary tools, resources, or programs that will intentionally develop the maturity you expect? For instance, are you allocating most of your resources to develop spiritual children rather than adults? Do you continue offering programs that seem outdated and ineffectual? Do you provide good programs that are underutilized? By scrutinizing current ministry methods, you can go back to the drawing board with more ideas on building a clearer ministry blueprint.

CHAPTER THREE

Transformation Versus Conformation

And we, who with unveiled faces all reflect the Lord's glory, are being transformed into his likeness with ever-increasing glory, which comes from the Lord, who is the Spirit.

2 Corinthians 3:18

C HILDREN LIVING IN our modern, fast-paced society are expected to grow up too fast. Events and experiences previously associated with the teen years now unfold in childhood. For instance, the Miss America Pageant has spun off versions of itself for younger and younger females. Today, competitions exist for Miss Teen and even Miss Toddler.

The pressure to participate and compete at earlier ages also affects sports. Teeball can seem like a professionals-only endeavor. Whatever happened to the low-key activities of childhood, like watching airplanes, kicking dirt, or playing sandlot baseball?

In the same way that society rushes kids to grow up, the church can shortcut the spiritual childhood phase—the bedrock phase of spiritual development mentioned in chapter 2. Church leaders can easily fall into the trap of taking new believers—especially those that have been successful in other areas of life—and catapulting them into service and prominence before they have been discipled to maturity. Not surprisingly, this approach often backfires. Yet the temptation lingers.

Consider the typical conversation between two church leaders as they discuss "Joe," a mutual acquaintance in the community. Within minutes, it becomes obvious that both view Joe as another E. F. Hutton: When he speaks, people listen. He is a powerful figure, a natural influencer. Unfortunately, Joe leads by intimidation and manipulation. Yet he gets things done, so most tolerate his questionable behavior and coarse language. "Wouldn't it be great if Joe would become a Christian?" they muse over cups of coffee. "Just think of what he could do if he were on our side serving God."

The Joe in your community could be a Jane who has made it to the top of her career. This woman has it all—success, charisma, poise, and class. What eye-catching billboards Joes and Janes could be for the cause of Christ! Nonetheless, wise church leaders need to disciple recently converted high-achievers with a crock pot—rather than a microwave—mentality.

Why? Because the heart of the discussion about a Joe or Jane revolves around the fuzzy idea that equates instant conformation with instant transformation. With God, new Christians can refocus their energy and clean up their behavior. The Holy Spirit can energize their talents and rearrange their priorities. However, too often the emphasis for new believers seems to be on external conformation, not radical internal transformation. After all, aren't we all basically good inside—especially if given the right environment?

In Romans 12:1-2, Paul taught the opposite: nothing short of complete transformation fits the plan of God for our lives. It helps to understand how the words "conform" and "transform" differ. "Conform" means "that which comprises the manner of life, actions." It involves changing the external. "Transform," on the other hand, comes from the Greek word *morphoo*, which influenced the English word "metamorphosis" and means "to change into another form." While the word "conformation" connotes external and transient change, "transformation" refers to a genuinely changed spiritual condition. Instead of wearing the appropriate Christian behaviors to conform, the transformed person's changed heart genuinely reveals itself in external virtues and behavior. True discipleship involves an inside-out process that takes time, a process that reminds me of my wife's Christmas sweet-roll preparation.

Each December, Mary makes these sweet rolls as a holiday tradition. They taste heavenly, and her annual baking effort is the only tradition I am adamant about keeping. Last year I watched her create her masterpiece again and noted that the end product looked very little like the ingredients lined up on our kitchen counter.

I observed that she created the dough with a number of ingredients and then mixed in a variety of nuts, fruits, and spices. She then rolled the dough, cut it into sections, and form-fitted those sections into a pan, which she placed into a preheated oven. After the recommended time passed, she pulled out the piping-hot rolls and—voila!—the doughy sections were transformed into fully baked Christmas sweet rolls!

The kids and I tend to attribute a sort of mystical greatness to my wife at these moments. But her success isn't really mysterious. She no more made the rolls than a farmer grows a crop.

Rather, Mary just knows the chemistry of this baking process. Every year she takes certain ingredients, mixes them together in a particular order, and then forms them in a specific shape. She realizes it takes heat and time to transform the raw materials into a finished product. We know this, too. That explains why we all wait for her to open the oven door and pull them out—ready at last.

Like this baking process, discipleship doesn't happen by accident. Rather, effective discipleship takes planning, time, and a certain amount of divine heat to transform someone into a fully baked follower of Christ.

However, well before that happens you've got to pull the

right ingredients together. The first ingredient is salvation, new birth in Christ. Another ingredient is the indwelling of the Holy Spirit, who works like yeast in the "baking" process of every believer. God's Word is still another critical ingredient of transformation. Finally, ongoing faith stands out as another indispensable ingredient—the desire and ability to trust and obey God more as we understand Him better (see Hebrews 11:6).

Matthew recorded one of the simplest ways Jesus called others to enter into the discipleship process: "Come, follow me . . . and I will make you fishers of men" (Matthew 4:19). Christ's call to discipleship was a call to change. The men Jesus addressed by the Sea of Galilee had been exposed to Him and His teaching in Judea, Samaria, and Galilee during that first year of His public ministry. They had seen His transforming power—the way He changed water into wine at Cana, the mind of the religious leader in Jerusalem, and the heart of a lonely woman at Sychar.

The call to transformation rang simply and clearly: Follow Me! Jesus didn't manipulate, plead, coerce, or argue. He didn't offer an escape from the pressures of normal living. Following Him didn't mean assuming a life of quiet contemplation or getting a theology degree. His associates came from the fringes of society, and His life and message were already officially suspect. So why would anyone respond to His call? Ultimately, some realized that to follow Christ was to apprentice under Him—the only perfect person to walk on Earth.

In *The Call*, Os Guinness wrote, "The deepest knowledge can never be put into words—or spelled out in sermons, books, lectures and seminars. It must be learned from the Master, under his authority, in experience."[1] Jesus called His disciples to walk with Him, to come, learn, imitate, and be transformed. Two thousand years later, His offer still stands.

Luke pointed out that "a student is not above his teacher, but everyone who is fully trained will be like his teacher" (Luke 6:40). The purpose of ministry involves making apprentices of Jesus. If you create enthusiasm for Him without transformation—essentially, congregations without apprentices—have you answered Christ's call?

The reality of life in God's kingdom must center on transformation, not conformation. In Colossians 1, Paul explains this dramatic change as a transfer from the kingdom of darkness to the kingdom of light. To be sure, life in the kingdom of light is unlike anything we have ever known. But being transferred from darkness to light only marks the beginning of the transforming reality of discipleship.

For one reason or another, humans have always hungered for new realities. On December 17, 1903, Orville and Wilbur Wright made history when they flew a heavier-than-air machine at Kitty Hawk, North Carolina. Though the flight covered only 120 feet (less that the wingspan of many modern aircraft), it opened a new reality that changed the human perspective forever.

Long after Galileo and Newton codified it, gravity still prevents us from entering the third dimension of space unaided. No wonder most learn at an early age to make peace with this basic law. On Earth, gravity remains a constant force at thirty-two feet per second squared. Both children and adults know that when you fall out of a tree, gravity always works. No mother worries that if her children jump too high they won't come down.

However, during the Enlightenment, pioneers like Newton and Bernoulli discovered another law: the law of lift. The new law of lift didn't eliminate the old law of gravity, but it countered it so that gravity lost its iron grip on our ankles. The Wright brothers, and every aeronautics engineer since, have understood and manipulated this law to get airborne.

This new law simply states that if air passes over a certain shape, an upward force is created, causing the shape—and whatever connects to it—to lift into that exhilarating space dimension. The law explains why gliders and jumbo jets fly and rocks don't. In a similar sense, Christians must be transformed—reshaped—in order to get the lift they need to experience the dynamic spiritual dimension.

Living in two dimensions (as we do on Earth) parallels living in the natural world without God. In this reality, spiritual gravity (sin) distorts the beauty of the two dimensional and makes everyone a prisoner of it. However, lift (the gospel or the Spirit of life) sets Christians free from the limitations and penalty of gravity to live now in 3-D (the added spiritual dimension).

Paul explains this concept in Romans 8:1-2: "Therefore, there is now no condemnation for those who are in Christ Jesus, because through Christ Jesus the law of the Spirit of life set me free from the law of sin and death."

More than one hundred years ago, Edwin Abbott wrote *Flatland*,[2] a book that shows how difficult it is to understand a new dimension as a person who has never experienced it —just as a person who has heard about the kingdom of God can't understand it without actually becoming a part of it.

Flatland is a two-dimensional world seen through the eyes of a square anthropomorphized as a scholarly and respectable gentleman. Living there is like living on the top of a table. There is length and width, but no height. One day, the square meets a sphere, and they clash on Flatland's reality. In their curious conversation, the sphere insists that actually three dimensions exist, not just two. As a sphere, this character knows about length and width as well as height. From his third dimension of height, the sphere explains that he can see "down" into the homes of Flatland—something the square cannot fathom.

Jesus came to us squares as a sphere. And, like the sphere in Flatland, He not only described life in 3-D, but also offered to lift us up and allow us to experience its reality. If that were not enough, He also revealed His plan to transform us to actually fit into the 3-D-like kingdom of God.

Interestingly, God originally designed humans as a three-dimensional—spiritual—part of the creation. People are unique in Godlikeness and the ability to relate to Him. But the human 3-D experience was short-lived.

Scripture explains that after Adam bit into the "apple," humanity lost its spiritual dimension with God and became a prisoner to two dimensions (see Genesis 3). The vacuum left in the human heart hints at this missing dimension. The

INTENTIONAL DISCIPLEMAKING

message of the kingdom says that we can be reborn to discover what was lost in the first Adam and reestablished in the second. Those in an intentional disciplemaking community will commit themselves to helping squarish Flatlanders experience the dimensions of spherehood.

Some seek what's missing through self-effort. But self-effort is really only a spiritual pogo stick. When I was in grade school, the pogo stick was as popular as the skateboard is today. We even had square dance lessons on pogo sticks in P.E. class. Kids loved this experience so much, they hopped around like kangaroos trying to set world records for jumping endurance. Why? Because when skillfully used, a pogo stick could put you in the third dimension for a couple of seconds. However, it could never sustain the break with gravity.

In the same way, self-effort alone can only offer short-lived breaks from spiritual gravity. Only true discipleship can supernaturally break the pull of spiritual gravity. Yet when Jesus announced that the transformational dimension of the kingdom of God was at hand, the Jews looked for a complete release from the push-and-pull associated with two-dimensional life. They wanted life to be more comfortable—an expectation that persists among Christians in modernity.

But spiritual transformation doesn't always make living in the two-dimensional natural world any easier. For instance, even those closest to Christ struggled to understand the implications of the kingdom of God and to live those out day by day. Indeed, pain, suffering, and loss even accompanied Christ's birth. Matthew explains that when the wise men failed to return to Herod with their report on the new king, life in two dimensions—especially around Bethlehem—got tougher, not easier. Mary and Joseph had to flee the country, leaving family, friends, and the familiar. In metro Bethlehem, other parents felt a different kind of pain. Herod, by decree, had mercilessly slaughtered all boys under the age of two in hopes of killing Jesus. (See Matthew 2:16-18.)

So, despite soaring with Christ in the third dimension, life in the other two dimensions continues to remind us of the gravity inherent in the fall of Adam and Eve. Even John the Baptist, a cousin of Jesus, understood this. Still, he served God well in spite of the difficult assignment to prepare the way for the Messiah, calling all to repentance *and* acting as the moral conscience of his people.

And he did a superb job! He received the highest honor possible from Christ, who said, "Among those born of women there has not risen anyone greater than John the Baptist" (Matthew 11:11). Wow! How impressive. Yet when John lands in prison for speaking up against immorality, where is Jesus? When a deviant king declares John's death sentence and the executioner is escorting John down the hall, where is Jesus?

Couldn't Jesus have sprung John from prison? After all, didn't Jesus announce that He had come to release captives? Would it have been too much for John to expect, after serving the cause of that all-important 3-D kingdom of God, to die of old age? We'll never know if John asked these questions, but I would have. I find myself thinking those thoughts when I'm camping and it rains. I reason that, after all I've done for God, is asking for a few days of sunshine too much?

Many people tend to have a consumer mentality that asks, "What can Jesus do for me?" Consequently, they feel disappointed when life doesn't necessarily get easier with Christ. Divorce still happens, cancer kills, companies downsize, and on and on. That's why life in two dimensions will never make sense by itself. It is only as you experience the call of Christ and follow Him into the kingdom of God that you will experience life as complete as it gets, pre-heaven.

Yet the life associated with the kingdom of God is not just a benefit when you die. It exists now. The only definition of eternal life that Christ gave is relational, as described in John 17:3: "Now this is eternal life: that they may know you, the only true God, and Jesus Christ, whom you have sent." Eternal life involves discipleship here on Earth— knowing Christ and following Him.

When Jesus began to teach about the transforming power of the kingdom of God, His audience naturally tried to interpret His message from a two-dimensional perspective. For instance, the Samaritan woman wanted the water

Christ offered so she would never need to draw water from a two-dimensional well again (see John 4:15). And in John 3, when Jesus told Nicodemus that eternal life required a new birth, Nicodemus initially tried picturing himself returning to a literal infancy.

Perhaps one of the greatest biblical examples of the tension between these realities is recorded in Matthew 19:16-26. It involves the young man who approached Jesus with a deep question: "What good thing must I do to get eternal life?" This is the first time the phrase "eternal life" is used in Matthew's gospel.

"If you want to enter life," Jesus replies, "obey the commandments." Jesus recognized that the man was not asking about some distant, futuristic, "when I die" life. He was asking about finding real life now.

The discussion progresses and Jesus gets to the core issue when He says, "If you want to be perfect, go, sell your possessions and give to the poor, and you will have treasure in heaven. Then come, follow me." Jesus contrasts the man's quest for heavenly treasure to discipleship. In other words, He didn't separate the man's eternal life from his life on Earth.

The man leaves, apparently unwilling to let go of his material security. And the apostles wrestle with the significance of what they have just heard. Before they can even verbalize their questions, Jesus gives an explanation: "It is easier for a camel to go through the eye of a needle than for a rich man to enter the kingdom of God." In this way, He makes seamless the connection between the issue of mortal life and eternal life, between discipleship and the kingdom of God.

In *The Divine Conspiracy*, Dallas Willard asks three key questions for discovering if this more holistic idea of transformation gets communicated by church leaders:[3]

- Does the gospel I preach and teach cause those who hear it to become full-time students of Jesus?
- Would those who believe it become His apprentices as a natural "next step"?

- What can we reasonably expect would result from people actually believing the substance of my message? (See again Matthew 19:16-26.)

As my wife and I sat through the grand performance of the sixth-grade summer music camp years ago, we tried to spot our son in the back row of the trombone section. When I found him, I waffled between two responses. The first was to stand up and shout, "That's my Barney!"—just like the father in *The Music Man*. The other response involved reflecting on the similarities this music scene had with discipleship. The latter seemed a wiser choice to pursue.

As the young musicians completed each song, the audience of parents, grandparents, and reluctantly attendant siblings erupted in clamorous applause. What were we applauding? Believe me, it wasn't a magnificent sound. Some of the young musicians had only recently learned how to put their instruments together, let alone play them.

We were not applauding a great performance—we were applauding change! After all, most of us had heard these same kids play in fifth grade. We were gratefully celebrating the change we heard. Though the instruments were different, the process remained the same.

We expected change. We encouraged it. We paid taxes to hire teachers that could facilitate it. We attended high school concerts so we would be reminded of what change could eventually sound like. We paid for music lessons and then endured endless hours of listening to our kids practice. We praised, challenged, and demanded musical discipline in spite of the reluctance, complaints, excuses, and tears our supervision elicited.

Initially, the motivation for our child to change was obviously external. Then, almost magically overnight, the drive for change became internal. The beginner's focus on scales, slide position, fingering, counting, and myriad other technical struggles gradually faded, and the music started flowing from within.

With this experience in mind, do you think the church

unwittingly spends most of its time promoting audience members rather than musicians? People can attend church and feel entertained, even impressed. Some leave with a wonderful warm feeling. But do they ever learn to play an instrument for themselves? Do they ever transform into true musicians who love to make music for God with others?

Spiritual transformation is like learning to play God's music through the instrument of your soul. Church leaders can't just throw everyone together in one large orchestra and expect a great performance. It requires intentional effort, combining knowledge, skill, practice, discipline, instruction, and encouragement. It requires individual skill and group participation. It requires the ability to follow the Conductor and to play together in tune. When it happens, it's beautiful. But only the ministry that plans for a transformed sound will ever hear it.

CHAPTER FOUR

Evangelism
Unpacked

> We are therefore Christ's ambassadors, as though God were making his appeal through us. We implore you on Christ's behalf: Be reconciled to God.
>
> 2 Corinthians 5:20

A PASTOR CALLED me the other day and asked for help in discipling people who, after coming forward during altar calls at his church, did not necessarily want to follow Christ or connect with the congregation. "We don't have trouble getting decisions," he explained. "We have trouble getting disciples." After discussing his ministry, I wondered if the problem was more in the church's evangelism approach than in its follow-up strategy.

Evangelism! I have observed three excellent ways for a person's heart rate to reach aerobic level quickly: jogging for thirty minutes, losing their two-year-old toddler while shopping in a blown glass retail store, or hearing the word "evangelism." Mention this subject, and many look for exit signs, feign headaches, or remember appointments that were never made. Nothing can bring terror, guilt, or just plain perspiration to the average Christian quicker than that topic. Why? Because typically, people associate evangelism with pushy used-car dealers, televangelists, door-to-door salespeople, crusaders, and so on.

When I ask church leaders how they think they can increase evangelism, the answer almost always involves hiring someone else to do that work. One senior pastor confided, "Our evangelism will take off when we can afford to hire someone gifted in evangelism who will set the pace for the rest of us." This is code for "I hope to get this monkey off my back so I can stick with teaching, which I love."

Other churches deal with this issue by scheduling a big event. Often they hire a well-known speaker who proclaims the gospel at a church men's breakfast, a women's luncheon, or a couples' potluck. Only a few members actually invite their neighbors (most don't know their neighbors), so the audience is made up of regular churchgoers with a few relatives who are in town for the weekend. Those who attend enjoy seeing their church friends again for the third time that week.

When George Barna summarized his research on evangelism in the video *The Ten Myths of Evangelism,* he reported as much. His book *Evangelism That Works* states that despite the 250 billion dollars spent annually on ministry by American churches, only one in eight church members feels prepared to share his or her faith. Barna also discovered that the typical church allocates only 2 percent of its gross annual revenues to evangelism.[1]

When the church does evangelize, it often measures its success in terms of the initial external displays of faith rather than by the deeper changes that stem from discipleship. Chapter 3 addresses this issue—the profound difference between conformation and transformation. Many church leaders eagerly count and report the baptisms, prayers, or number of response cards that result from event-oriented evangelism. However, because only God knows a person's heart and only God brings conversion, we will always measure evangelism's impact with some degree of uncertainty.

While there is a place in the evangelism process for hosting big events and using response indicators, they remind me of my early "pass-through" evangelism method.

This strategy involved sowing broadly, reaping the reapable, and quickly moving on.

Big events fit the transient university culture where I first received evangelism training. There my colleagues and I aimed to expose as many people to the gospel as possible. With forty thousand students on campus and Jesus' statement fixed in our minds—"Behold, I say to you, lift up your eyes, and look on the fields, that they are white for harvest" (John 4:35, NASB)—we looked for the harvest! We even figured out a statistically realistic harvest yield. If you shared the gospel with ten people, one would inevitably become a Christian.

The sheer population of the university mission field, combined with the fact that ten thousand new students showed up every year, created endless opportunities. So we found those interested in seeking God and spent time with them.

In addition, our mission-minded para-church organization sponsored debates on the topic of God and held rallies at which professors and athletes shared their testimonies. In this way, we excitedly watched hundreds of students come to Christ.

The apostle Paul practiced a similar pass-through strategy. He would pass through a city, preach the gospel, reap a harvest, set up a church, and travel to the next community. His calling and motivation centered on preaching the gospel where it had never been preached. Nevertheless, when he instructed the early church in evangelism, he did not teach them to emulate this method. Instead, he primarily taught them to penetrate the local culture and make disciples.

In some settings, the pass-through evangelism strategy still works. However, regardless of the mobility of the American culture, most of the population lives in communities that have a sense of permanence. Buying a home still represents a big chunk of the American Dream. Therefore, a penetration approach—not a pass-through approach—works best.

I could not completely appreciate this until I worked as an aeronautical engineer for Boeing Aircraft in Seattle. After the company placed me in an electronics division assigned to enhance the 747 jumbo jet, I quickly realized that the ten people in my division didn't fit the pass-through profile. Rather, I anticipated working with them for years. If I used a strategy of "sow broadly, reap the reapable, and move on," it would have been a lonely, fruitless tenure.

Unfortunately, some churches still promote a pass-through evangelism strategy in the context of stable, fairly permanent communities. This ultimately isolates the church from society and encourages a fortress mentality—the absolute antithesis of evangelism. In fact, using the pass-through strategy in settled communities makes it very easy for lost people to escape the influence of the church. All they have to do is turn down the invitation to the pass-through-style event.

If they say "no thanks" to an invitation, they become indefinitely out of reach. On the other hand, when a church evangelizes with a penetration strategy of ongoing love, relationship, and service, it's much tougher for nonChristians to ignore the church's gospel message.

In *Follow Me*,[2] Jan Hettinga explains that the gospel is not just a gift to be received, but a new leader to follow. Given the increasingly biblically illiterate public, the Christian community needs to do more than merely expose those outside of the church to the gospel. It needs to patiently help those within and without to understand it more fully in community. That, too, can be a critical part of the evangelism process because it represents a return to the roots of Christian faith.

The big event of Pentecost launched the first-century church, and spiritual gifts such as preaching and teaching often equip people to lead revivals today. Yet the first generation of Christians certainly did not view evangelism as an event-driven experience executed by the precious few with that gift. Rather, evangelism and discipleship took place among "ungifted" people through many small events and encounters.

And good thing! The church needs a team—a community of people—to be effective. No one person embodies all the gifts, and understanding this concept helps a church

INTENTIONAL DISCIPLEMAKING

discover a new freedom to work as a union of parts with each member using his or her gifting in the evangelism/discipleship process. Fact is, the more a church focuses on reaching the lost, the greater the need for those with gifts that offer mercy and encourage relationship. These gifts in particular help the church to better demonstrate the love of Christ to a secular, postmodern world.

In this way, the church can capitalize on strengths and help each member find freedom to serve in the way God has wired him or her. Interestingly, when I lead evangelism workshops, I frequently ask for those who think they are gifted in that area to raise their hands. In one seminar, only seven out of the seventy there raised their hands. Out of those seven, four had not shared their faith with anyone in the past two years. Of the remaining three, two had shared their faith only once. The response never passes 10 percent—and that's from a crowd interested in the subject![3]

Regardless of the percentage of gifted evangelists in any church, there will never be enough to build a strategy around. We need models that connect with the other 90-plus percent of the church in order to impact the world for Christ. Thankfully, evangelism can begin with anyone who has a dynamic relationship with Jesus Christ.

Most evangelism training focuses on teaching a Christian how to share his or her own faith story and how to explain the gospel. But a single individual never accomplishes the whole process of evangelism in isolation. Evangelism remains a function of the body of Christ, which reflects a utilization of gifts and a division of labor.

My wife, Mary, discovered this dynamic a few years ago when she met Linda, a cosmetic consultant concerned about reaching her lost friends. As they got to know each other, they realized that God had given them complementary gifts that could enhance their outreach. So Mary used her gift of teaching while Linda used her gift of hospitality to set up some small-group Bible discussions on relevant issues for women. Linda recruited and Mary led the discussions. Together they were able to do what neither could do alone.

When I read Luke's report on Philip's encounter with the Ethiopian (see Acts 8:26-39), I often wonder how many people were involved in this stranger's journey to faith in Christ. Whom did he encounter at the temple on his recent visit? Where did he first develop an interest in the monotheistic Jewish faith?

I find great encouragement in Paul's message to the Corinthians, "The man who plants and the man who waters have one purpose, and each will be rewarded according to his own labor" (1 Corinthians 3:8). I imagine we will be surprised when one day God evaluates the labor and elevates both the sowers and the cultivators to the gold-medal stand.

In John 17, Jesus prays that the unity of believers will point outsiders to His reality. We should never underestimate the power that comes from establishing loving, productive relationships within the body and exposing seekers to them. The absence of such relationships may explain at least one barrier to effective evangelism in today's church.

A loving, disciplemaking church maximizes effectiveness by learning more about how nonChristians think and feel. (On this subject, I found books like *Inside the Mind of Unchurched Harry and Mary* by Lee Strobel[4] and *The Frog in the Kettle* by George Barna[5] insightful.) This type of church also recognizes that three broad categories of nonChristians exist: the lost within the church, the lost who will visit the church, and the lost who will not visit the church. This awareness enables more effective outreach.

The Lost Within the Church

The church will always contain those that are lost. No matter how structured the membership screening, there will always be some who know the right answers, but lack a personal relationship with Christ. In *Evangelism That Works*, George Barna concluded that half of those who attend Protestant churches on a typical Sunday morning have not accepted Christ as Savior.[6]

Jesus told a parable regarding the mix of weeds and

wheat in the kingdom of God. One day God will judge and separate the authentic from the counterfeit as described in Matthew 13:24-30. In the meantime, depending on the personality and history of your church, you must find a way to address this group—no easy task considering they are comfortable in church culture—and lovingly clarify the gospel.

The Lost Who Will Visit the Church

The second category describes the unchurched who will visit a church. People in this group may be considered "pre-churched" because they have some type of church reference point. For instance, they may have attended church as children. These individuals at some point probably concluded that church was irrelevant to their adult lives, so they left it behind like their high school letter jackets. Often, pre-churched people eventually return as young parents seeking help in establishing a moral foundation for their children.

"I don't need this religion," they reason, "but my kids do. I can make it, but I am worried about them. After all, a little religious morality can't hurt."

Sometimes the pre-churched give God and church a second chance when work, family, or financial situations turn out to be less than what they had planned. When disap pointment clouds their dreams, when they feel out of solutions, they may hope that something has changed at the church of their childhood—that this time there will be real answers to life's big questions.

These people carry a casual biblical worldview. God is in their moral framework, though distant and impersonal. Typically, women sense the need to reconnect with God and the church before men do. They are the ones who initiate bringing the family through the church doors. In this case, the church nursery and children's classes are important factors in influencing the decision to return. It helps if the environment is upbeat, friendly, and attractive—and if the kids enjoy the experience.

Many churches intentionally orient Sunday morning services to meet the needs of this group of people. These churches refer to themselves as seeker oriented, seeker targeted, or seeker sensitive. Willow Creek Community Church near Chicago stands out as the flagship church for this strategy.

A seeker-sensitive Sunday morning service is one strategy to reach this group. But it isn't the only one, nor will it fit every church. In many cases, the Sunday worship service will not be a key part of the outreach strategy. Rather, leaders will continue designing it as a worship time for the family of God. Outsiders are always welcome, but not a priority. Other churches will lean on a small-group program to make a less intimidating entry point. Many possibilities exist.

The Lost Who Will Not Visit the Church

Finally, some people—for whatever reason—will never visit a church. They may express an interest in God or spirituality, but they have decided that church is irrelevant to their worldview. If there are spiritual answers to life's big questions, these people are convinced that they won't find them at church. It doesn't matter how big the loudspeakers are, how snappy the marquee looks, or how big the church's newspaper ad is. These folks will not attend your church meeting.

They remind me of hikers lost in the mountains, while the church reminds me of a community operating in the valley. Many of the lost in this category come from parents and even grandparents who also got lost in the mountains. Several generations have never been to the valley of the churches. They don't even get married in churches.

A few years ago, while watching television, I flipped to a true story that had been made into a television special entitled *Snowbound*. The drama revolved around a young couple and their baby who got lost trying to cross the mountains in northern California on their way to Idaho. Despite the heavy snowstorm, Jim and Jenny Stolpa took an alternative route when the highway patrol closed the interstate.

Not surprisingly, they became snowbound on a lonely road fifty miles from the nearest town. They had no provisions and no means of communication. After four days of waiting in their truck for help, they almost lost hope. As a last resort, they decided to walk eighteen miles over the mountains in search of a road they had discovered on their map. After walking all day and night in deep snow, they still found no sign of a road.

Meanwhile, their parents had aggressively marshaled all of the resources at their disposal to help search for their children and grandchild. The police, Forest Service, and news media all teamed up to rescue the stranded family. However, despite the commitment and skill of this group, their efforts turned out to be frustratingly ineffective because they faced two major limitations. First, they had to search thousands of square miles of mountainous terrain. Second, continuous winter storms made aerial and ground reconnaissance impossible anyway.

Jim and Jenny, now lost for six days, decided to split in order to survive. While Jenny and the baby waited in a small cave, Jim returned to their abandoned truck hoping to backtrack from there to the nearest town.

On the eighth day of this ordeal, as Jim was stumbling down a deserted, snow swept road, a cattle rancher spotted him. The rancher immediately took the dehydrated and frostbitten man to his mountain cabin. Before Jim was taken down the mountain to a local hospital, the rancher got a faint description of the route he had taken from the cave.

The rancher and a few of his friends then set out in a blizzard to find Jenny and the baby. Ultimately, Jim's sketchy description, combined with the knowledge of a local ranger, provided the clues for a miraculous rescue.

Spiritually lost people get trapped in the mountains, too—in the snowdrifts of secularism, skepticism, and narcissism. Due to foolish choices or unfortunate circumstances, they get hopelessly separated from the rescue efforts of those that live in the valley.

Furthermore, valley people often are unaware or uninterested in the fate of those lost in the mountains. Valley people are too busy doing healthy valley things that take their time and energy. Some hear about the lost people in the mountains and try to help. Some bring blankets and set up aid stations. Some write articles and make videos of the dangers of mountain travel. Some actually try to fly over the mountains and drop supplies.

But to reach those trapped in the mountains of our secular society, the church must create a radically alternative route that requires both caring local ranchers and rangers skilled at negotiating the terrain. It will also take teams of courageous search parties that are aware of who's lost and equipped to handle the many discouraging obstacles.

The book of Acts explains that the early church found much of its success through the centrifugal force spinning from Jerusalem. And much of the New Testament records how Jesus changed the direction of evangelism forever with His "go to the mountains" approach.

However, in the Old Testament the Jews used a primarily centripetal model of sharing God with others. It was a "come to" strategy. Build a grand temple, demonstrate the moral and civil laws of the Lord, and the nations will notice and draw near.

Peter's audience in Acts 2 was an exception rather than the norm. That audience resulted from the centripetal force of people being drawn into the religious center, the temple. Peter then simply capitalized on this gathered audience and appealed to their religious heritage with a message that touched their collective consciousness.

Despite Christ's "go to" approach to meeting the lost and making disciples of them, very few contemporary churches reach outside their four walls. In *Church Without Walls*, Jim Petersen points out that some churches operate using the lingering "come and listen" strategy as if they still serve a largely rural and illiterate society.[7]

Stewardship issues represent another reason building-centered evangelism persists. Because so much of a church's resources go into the structure, members feel it should be well used. But the evangelistic pursuits of Jesus and the disciples were very mobile and flexible. In fact—according to James Rutz in *The Open Church*—it wasn't until the fourth century during the reign of Roman emperor Constantine that church buildings and "Christian" architecture developed.[8]

Another inward force is comfort. The church environment often represents a safe home to Christians, and we feel others would surely feel the same way. That the unchurched would find our church building unattractive, intimidating, awkward, or just weird is a difficult pill to swallow.

As a couple trying to relate to neighbors and unchurched friends, Mary and I soon realized that even our home was not the first place to begin a relationship. When we invite new people to spend time with us these days, it usually involves neutral ground like a restaurant or perhaps a backyard cookout.

The inside of our home, much less a church building, is simply not neutral ground for the unchurched. For this reason, planning evangelistic activities "on campus" creates an unnecessary barrier for many of the lost. To overcome that barrier, we need to sacrifice our comfort to figure out where the unchurched would feel more at ease.

Ultimately, how Christians view lost people will determine the motivation to remove barriers—buildings or otherwise—to the gospel. My early evangelism training often referred to the process of evangelism as going to war. We were in a battle and invading Satan's territory. Prayer was critical, as we needed the full armor of God. Up to that point, the theology held water. But sometimes we would casually refer to lost people as the enemy who we were out to capture. The lost were rebels who needed to be conquered.

I eventually realized that the enemy imagery described Satan—not the lost. When Jesus announced His mission in His hometown of Nazareth, He described the lost as blind, downcast, and captives (see Isaiah 61:1-2 and Luke 4:18-19). At other times, He referred to them as the sick in need of a physician or as sheep in need of a shepherd (see Matthew 9:12 and Luke 15:3-6). Finally, in 2 Corinthians 4:3-4 Paul refers to lost people as the dead in need of life and the blind in need of sight.

There is certainly nothing threatening about these descriptions. So instead of feeling hostility, I now feel compassion. Rather than feeling defensive, I feel empathy, which is a very authentic place to start in the evangelism process.

CHAPTER FIVE

Overcoming
Barriers

Sow your seed in the morning, and at evening let
not your hands be idle, for you do not know which
will succeed, whether this or that, or whether both
will do equally well.

Ecclesiastes 11:6

O NCE A DISCIPLEMAKING community recognizes
the three groups of lost people described in chapter 4 —
the lost within the church, the lost who will visit the church,
and the lost who won't visit the church — it needs to focus
intently on overcoming barriers. The three main barriers in
order of difficulty are the volitional barrier (the will), the
intellectual barrier, and the emotional barrier.

To understand these barriers and how best to overcome
them, I use a castle metaphor. Wealthy landowners in
medieval Europe built castles for security and protection.
Ideally, they surrounded them with moats as a first level of
defense. A drawbridge could be lowered from the castle gate
to allow access to those considered friendly. The castle walls
provided the second level of defense. Of course, the higher
and thicker the walls, the better the security. A main gate
served as the point of access. The final barrier was the tower.
No wonder royal families lived there!

In terms of spiritual vulnerability, many people's lives look like this feudal picture. Because they rule their castle, the flag that flies over it is the flag of ego or self. Self-rule — independence from God — is at the heart of that person's identity. However, those who have submitted to Christ fly a new flag over their castle, indicating their allegiance to a new king.

Evangelism attempts to get each castle owner to lower his or her flag and raise the banner of Christ in its place. Disciplemaking communities can then step in and address the implications of this new leadership. After all, when Christ governs castle life, the dethroned occupant must undergo the slow process of acquiring new values, beliefs, and behaviors that please the King.

When church leaders strategize on how to get to the tower, they can use two approaches. The first, a military mentality, involves attacking the castle to break down the walls, bash in the gate, and overpower the defense. The other approach begins with relating to the castle ruler in such a way that he or she will eventually let down the drawbridge, open the gate, and invite access to the tower.

Let's focus on the second approach, which could be called process evangelism. This approach minimizes the defenses that are erected when people feel threatened. In this case, the emotional barrier — the moat — is overcome when a Christian builds a bridge of love that touches the castle owner's heart. This bridge must ultimately be strong enough to bear the weight of truth. The bridge of love builds trust, allowing people to feel safe and enabling them to listen to a message that ultimately confronts and convicts. The bridge must also safely stretch over the isolation, suspicion, fear, and hostility swimming in the moat like sharks.

Once the Christian has bridged the emotional barrier, he or she will face the steep castle wall, which represents the intellectual barrier. At the foot of the wall, it's important to spark the owner's interest in King Jesus. Questions and answers may make it seem like just another information session, but the purpose of conversing at this wall is to help the owner understand the truth of the information. If that happens, the owner will open the heavy iron-braced gates.

Inside the castle, the Christian can see the winding tower steps and knows that only the volitional barrier remains. God's grace, combined with the Christian witness, may eventually lead the castle owner to repentance. That's when he or she will raise a new flag in place of—not alongside—the old one.

Bridging the Emotional Moat

In this first endeavor, the choice of materials is critical to the success of bridge building. Typically, crews build bridges out of steel, concrete, and wood. The solid materials in relationships are trust, respect, and credibility. This means you are approachable, believable, and authentic. In relationships, bridges can be built in a matter of moments, but it usually takes time.

The bridges you build may not get you over the moat, but they may be strong enough to support someone else crossing step by step with the weight of God's truth. That explains why in process evangelism there are no insignificant contacts.

In your daily life, you may not always share the gospel, but you can keep building bridges. Remember that every encounter with lost people, whether spontaneous or planned, is a chance to enter the evangelism process.

Shopping at the local Wal-Mart takes on new significance when you see yourself as a bridge builder for Christ. The clerk no longer looks like an animated scanning operator, but like the ruler of a castle that may need a bridge built.

To begin, identify your God-given networks. Whom do you relate to most comfortably? Then try to appreciate that evangelism can happen wherever God places you. New relationships can be found where you work and live, where you play, in your family, and through divine appointments.

As you explore each network, ask yourself this question: "Whom is God placing on my heart for heaven?" Not every person in your workplace will respond to you, or you to them. You will not find common ground with every resident in your neighborhood. But all these networks make great places to start looking.

Take some time to pray about the people in these various networks. Make a list of three to four of them that God seems to have put on your heart. If you are part of a small group or lead a small group, encourage others to develop a list of people God has put on their heart and begin to pray for them, too.

After you have identified your network, interact. Begin relating to those with whom you share common activities and interests. Note that without seeking those with shared interests, you will probably fail in your bridge-building mission. Three factors will increase your effectiveness as a bridge builder: intentionality, consolidation, and pliability.

Intentionality

Successful interaction requires intentionality. Rather than passively waiting for opportunities to develop, you need to take the initiative. Set up the neighborhood block party. Invite your office mate to a baseball game. Offer to baby-sit your neighbors' kids so they can enjoy a weekend away.

Intentionality develops as we pray for specific people, as we relate on common ground, as we meet real needs, and as we share our lives authentically. Bridge building cannot be done without this contact. If it's a priority, this kind of involvement will take time and sacrifice. Wondering how you can add more activities to an already busy schedule?

Consolidation

Consolidation is one solution. Rather than creating separate activities for bridge-building evangelism, integrate those experiences into what you already do.

Jim worked in an office with thirty other people. As we talked about who was on his heart for heaven, four to five men came to mind. The problem was that they lived in different parts of the city, and his only contact was at work. Jim's young family and a heavy work schedule left little time for new activities. I asked Jim what he did for lunch. Lunch was the one leisure time he could share with those men. It didn't require any special scheduling or travel.

Jim explained that he usually used his lunch break to catch up on paperwork. The office emptied at noon, and he could focus uninterrupted. He felt his habit was an efficient use of time because he could eat at his desk and fill out the forms in peace. However, as we conversed, he recognized that by making a few minor adjustments, he could practice consolidation. He started going to lunch with one of the men on his heart once a week.

Pliability

Successful bridge building also involves pliability. People are more receptive to spiritual issues at special times. This reminds me of my efforts in shaping the clay in my backyard. The ground is either too wet or too dry to level. When it's wet, it is sticky and forms clumps that are hard to remove from shoes, shovels, and kids. When it's dry, it is like hardened concrete. I realize that there is a short window of time when I can work with this soil—usually about two days in the spring and two days in the fall!

People are like this clay. You can never predict when someone's heart will be sensitized to spiritual things. It may result from a job layoff, an illness, or a soccer championship. That's why it's important to stay connected—to be ready to build bridges during those rare pliable moments when people are the most spiritually sensitive.

Entering the Intellectual Fortress

Entrance through the castle wall only happens when the castle owner explores truth—spiritual truth. To encourage this exploration, spiritual topics first must be introduced at some point. During this introduction stage, it's important to bring biblical truth to life values. These conversations must go beyond news, weather, sports, and kids to life values and needs. (By the way, if you're not comfortable talking about life values, you won't be comfortable sharing the gospel.) Try delving below facts to feelings and beliefs. This opens the door to sharing biblical truth on life issues. These introductions can be formal or informal, planned or spontaneous.

Remember that like Christians, nonChristians are trying to put life together. They do the best they can with what they have. They just do not have all the pieces. This common ground of putting life together allows you to share the relevance of biblical truth and the way that truth has impacted your life.

In *Evangelism Through the Local Church*, Michael Green writes,

> Not many people are brought to Christ via the route of the intellect, though some are. Vital though the intellect is, most people are won when they sense Christ coming to touch broken places and torn feelings in their lives.[1]

After introducing spiritual topics, the second stage of entering the intellectual fortress involves inviting people to discuss the gospel and other issues from the Bible. Ultimately, you must introduce seekers to Jesus—His claims and teaching. Equipping people to investigate and discover Christ in this stage of evangelism may require a variety of tools. *Jesus Cares for Women* by Helene Ashker (NavPress, 1989) and my book *Design 4 Discovery* (The Navigators Church Discipleship Ministry, 1993) offer ways to stimulate discovery and investigation. And both can be used individually or in small groups.

Climbing the Volitional Tower

The third and most powerful barrier to faith is the will. The focus of this stage of evangelism is persuasion—helping the castle owner convert to a personal faith. This is the anticipated part of the journey where God, by grace through faith, creates new life.

This process often unfolds in two stages as well. The

INTENTIONAL DISCIPLEMAKING

first stage, the illustration stage, involves presenting an easily understood gospel summary. After Jesus illustrated who He was to the disciples, He stopped and gave a quiz: "Who do the crowds say I am?" He asked. Jesus' second question was more personal, "Who do *you* say I am?" (Luke 9:18,20, emphasis added). Though the crowd's understanding was still incomplete, they had come to some important conclusions. So when you illustrate the gospel, aim to help the seeker put the big-picture pieces together as the Holy Spirit brings conviction and faith.

"When all you have is a hammer, you'll treat everybody like a nail," goes the adage. By developing an expanding toolbox of presentation illustrations, you can personalize this message with the people you meet.

Illustrating the gospel in a visual summary form leads naturally to the second stage of climbing the volitional tower—inquiry. Inquiry happens when a Christian asks a seeker about his or her spiritual journey. This approach gives the seeker an opportunity—and some incentive—to take the next step. The next step may be to repent and receive Christ by faith. Or it could simply be to move another step closer to Christ. Inquiry can be as simple as asking, "In light of what you have just seen in this illustration, where would you say you are in your journey to God?"

There are only three responses that people have to the gospel. In process evangelism, we need to know how to recognize and handle each. Paul experienced these three responses when he delivered his message on Mars Hill (see Acts 17:22-34). One group responded by sneering. They thought Paul was crazy or the message was strange or both. They were not ready to buy into what he preached. They obviously needed more time and exposure. Both the emotional and intellectual barriers needed to be penetrated before Paul could even think of getting through their volitional barrier.

Another group said, "We want to hear you again on this subject." They were curious, but not convinced. They were seekers who needed more investigation and discovery experiences. People at this stage of coming to Christ need opportunities to explore gospel issues. You must spend time overcoming the intellectual barrier by engaging them in truth investigations.

The third response Paul got was "some men joined him and believed" (verse 34, NASB). God had opened their hearts. Individuals in this group believe or they want to believe. Helping these people formulate their decision by praying is an exciting moment in process evangelism.

Often, however, seekers come to faith along the journey and don't tell you until later. Larry had been discussing the Bible with his seeker friend Bob for months before he noticed a change in him. One day, instead of referring to "what you believe" and "your Bible," Bob began referring to "what *we* believe" and "*our* Bible." Upon further inquiry, Bob said that a few weeks earlier he had responded to Christ by faith after one of his discussions with Larry.

Most evangelism training focuses on individual efforts like Larry's, and the assumption is that Larry should be able to overcome each barrier equally well. For instance, Larry should be as capable of building bridges over the emotional barrier as he is at scaling the volitional tower. While individual evangelism training certainly is a key part of any outreach strategy, greater effectiveness comes from joining others in team or corporate outreaches.

Team Outreach

Many churches use small groups for nurturing and caregiving. They have experienced the benefits of a small group focused on a common objective. The same benefits result as teams practice evangelism. Teams invite people to exercise their strengths while benefiting from the strengths of others. Teams also encourage accountability and sharpen the group's focus on this critical ministry.

As a team, two or more people simply decide to be more deliberate about bringing Christ to a lost person's castle. They work together to overcome the barriers of emotion, intellect, and will. Rather than just an individual modeling Christian faith, the team becomes the model in addition to the individuals within it.

Jesus appreciated the team dynamic. After all, He formed twelve men into an identifiable band focused on His mission. Even in their early training, Jesus didn't send the disciples out as individuals but in pairs. Paul used teams to take the gospel to the Gentile world. If you want to reach a modern culture increasingly isolated from the church, you'll need teams.

After reading *Conspiracy of Kindness*[2] by Steve Sjogren, one church formed an evangelism team to focus on new neighborhood residents overwhelmed with unpacking and getting settled. This team offered to rake, mow, and trim to make life a little less hectic for them. They charged nothing. There were no strings attached to this service and no agenda other than to show the love of Christ in a tangible way. In this way, teams can build strong bridges over the emotional moat of people's lives.

Teams can also enter the intellectual fortress. Small-group discussions on relevant issues like marriage, children, and finances can be done as a team in the marketplace, a neighborhood, or a church. Some teams offer recovery groups to interest seekers in exploring the Christian community and the Bible's answers to real life issues. These teams understand that, in the context of a caring small group, seekers can more easily move from spiritual felt needs to the gospel.

In Columbia, Missouri, some businessmen effectively use team outreach to enter otherwise closed intellectual fortresses. Once a month they meet for a Discovery Forum at a businessman's home. Each team member brings his seeker friends to meet other men and discuss relevant issues from the Bible. In this environment, those skilled in teaching and leading discussions use their strengths while those gifted in hospitality add their part. In this way, the team successfully exposes seekers to the dynamic unity of Christ's body.

A few years ago I had the privilege of working with Bob and Betty Jacks, a couple who has successfully modeled evangelism through the team model. The Jacks call their team concept "Your Home a Lighthouse."[3] In this model, a team gathers around a common mission and strategy. They organize a Bible study for nonChristians where one of the couples hosts, another leads the discussion, and everybody invites friends.

Teams can also scale the volitional tower where, for the nonChristian, the flag of self flies. For instance, my wife joined a team that hosted a Christmas tea. This small group of women sponsored a cookie exchange during the holidays and invited friends to a home to share recipes and discuss the Christmas story. The speaker shared a simple gospel message and invited the women to respond by signing a card indicating their interest in receiving Christ or knowing more. This team initiated follow-up based on the responses.

Developing teams like this for evangelism takes planning, effort, and creativity. But once people experience the benefits of teamwork, they will never be content to minister alone again.

Corporate Outreach

Corporate outreach includes the typical "city crusade" or church evangelistic event where a speaker shares the gospel with a large group. The fruitfulness of this event depends on the rest of the matrix; when individual and team dynamics are not in place, corporate outreaches are usually fairly sterile — they don't reproduce believers.

One church in Tulsa, Oklahoma, used a corporate outreach as a bridge-building event by sponsoring a landscaping workshop for the subdivision in their area. The church sat in the midst of a growing part of the city, and many moving in were not familiar with the climate. The church-sponsored "Landscaping in Oklahoma" seminar and barbecue turned out to be like a neighborhood block party. In this way, the church established relationships, met needs, and shared the love of Christ in a practical way. Nobody presented the gospel. It was purely a bridge-building event.

Another church in Kansas City hired a professional comedy sports team to perform in the community one evening. This, too, made a great family-oriented, bridge-building event. That church designed this corporate outreach as a fun way to relate to those who would not initially come to a church service.

Most churches have members with expertise in areas of felt need. A church in St. Louis created a corporate outreach that shared the skills and gifts of the family counselors in the church. Ultimately, the church hosted a two-hour seminar on building a successful marriage. Riding on the popularity of John Gray's book *Men Are from Mars, Women Are from Venus,* the church entitled the seminar "Help, I Married an Alien!"

The church used the local high school auditorium so members could bring their unchurched friends to a neutral environment. Biblical principles were shared, but not in religious language. After the seminar, many went to homes or restaurants to discuss the topic and build bridges.

But be forewarned. As you plan both corporate outreaches and team-related gatherings, remember that nothing will undermine the momentum of evangelism more quickly than violating the integrity and purpose of the event. A few years ago, some women discovered success using team dynamics. So they sought to add corporate outreach to their evangelism efforts. They planned a luncheon with a fashion show and invited a speaker to share on a relevant life issue in a nonthreatening, seeker-friendly way. The team recruited other church women to invite their unchurched acquaintances to this event. To their dismay, everyone understood the purpose of the meeting—except the speaker. Instead of giving a principle-oriented message designed for those unfamiliar with the Bible, the speaker delivered a strong Bible teaching. The content was excellent and appropriate for seminary students, but not for seekers. Because the women had a different expectation when they invited their friends, they felt ambushed. Imagine how difficult it will be to gain the trust of those seekers when the church plans the next event.

Mining the Vein

Finally, regardless of which method you use, one of your greatest challenges will be keeping the gospel mobile—finding ways to bring it to castles near and far. To achieve more mobility and effectiveness with less effort takes a certain mindset. I call it "mining the vein," and it involves working smarter—not harder—in individual, team, and corporate evangelism.

I started using this phrase a few years ago after a family camping excursion in the Rocky Mountains of southern Colorado. One of the highlights involved four-wheeling in the backcountry, where we spotted some abandoned silver mines above the timberline. Closer up, we noticed that unnatural piles of yellowish rock usually marked mine entrances.

Surveying one mine, I wondered why the prospector dug there when he had thousands of acres of mountain terrain from which to choose. Why did he pick this slope and not the one further over? Tourist literature explained that prospectors dug rather blindly and hoped to eventually hit a vein of silver deeper within the mountain, a seam that would lead them to a "mother lode" of precious metal.

The crusty old prospector was not interested in creating myriad mine entrances to impress later generations. He wanted silver—and lots of it. So he focused on locating and following veins in his area of the Rocky Mountains. Evangelism has its own "mining the vein" strategy, but too often Christians stay busy creating mine entrances rather than following the veins they have already found. Jesus modeled the "mining the vein" principle in reaching Matthew. At that time, Matthew was like silver in rough ore form trapped in the mountains—a misfit rejected by the mainstream religious people. If Jesus had held Bible studies in the temple, Matthew wouldn't have attended. He wouldn't have known about the Bible study or cared about going—until Jesus found him and asked him to follow.

Through His relationship with Matthew, Jesus got access

to other mountain people. So Matthew was the mine entrance, and Christ's mobility and flexibility allowed Him to find other disciples in the shaft.

A few years ago, Mary and I discipled a couple well outside of our socioeconomic and religious comfort zone. The relationship seemed like a divine encounter only God could create. One day, they invited us to lead a Bible study in their home for them and a few other couples in their social circle. The group cautiously accepted us at first. But eventually, we gained their trust and respect. And in this way—because we had been willing to explore the vein, not just the mine entrance—we developed a whole new network otherwise hidden from our view.

Unfortunately, the church tends to take the initial silver discovery and bring it back down the mountain rather than continue digging in the same location. This results in many tunnel entrances without much silver.

CHAPTER SIX

Discipleship Dynamics

And the things you have heard me say in the presence of many witnesses entrust to reliable men who will also be qualified to teach others.

2 Timothy 2:2

G OLF HAS EXPLODED on the American sports scene in recent years with stars like the amazing Tiger Woods. The senior golf tour has stirred more interest as has the Ladies Professional Golf Association. To top it all off, the recently completed Golf Hall of Fame in St. Augustine, Florida, now celebrates the sport's history with an official institution.

Surely part of golf's popularity and intrigue stems from its universal appeal. Everyone can play it—young and old, men and women, athletic and nonathletic. Past hockey players with bad knees, retired basketball players with bad backs, and wannabe jocks who never made the big time can take on golf and find some success.

While this diverse group enjoys playing golf, sometimes to the level of fanaticism, another group finds it unspeakably dull. Hitting a round ball through the woods—or worse yet, watching others hit it through the woods—seems as exciting as watching paint dry. If you belong to this group, bear with me as I draw a parallel between developing one's golf game and creating an intentional disciplemaking church.

There are three types of clubs in the golf bag that need to be mastered to develop an intentional disciplemaking church. Roughly speaking, there are the drivers, the irons, and the putter. Each club has advantages and limitations. Skilled golfers not only know how to use each club, but also know how to select the right club for each shot.

The drivers or "woods"—so called either due to the historic wooden head and shaft or because that's where most people wind up when they use them—give the golfer the greatest opportunity to achieve distance. Unfortunately, a small degree of initial inaccuracy produces an exaggerated error at the end of the shot, so using drivers typically means sacrificing accuracy for distance. The irons, on the other hand, provide increased control in lieu of respectable distance. Finally, the most accurate club available is the putter; but it works best only within very short distances.

Jesus mandated disciplemaking, something that always happens within three relational dynamics—large groups, small groups, and life to life. These relational dynamics parallel golf clubs in that each one has strengths and limitations. And, like a skilled golfer, the intentional disciplemaking community benefits from learning when and how to use each one most effectively. Some ministries favor one and ignore the others. But for maximum impact, it's important to understand and play with all three.

Large Groups: The Driver

Large groups are made up of seventy people or more. And interestingly, the large-group dynamic remains roughly the same in groups of one hundred as in groups of ten thousand or more. Why? Because in large groups, the majority are simply spectators. This environment unavoidably limits participation and intimacy. Yet it can also inspire, inform, and motivate.

Historically, large-group dynamics have been effective in triggering the first phase of the discipleship process. For instance, in the eighteenth century, George Whitefield and

John Wesley effectively led evangelistic crusades for the same reasons Billy Graham led them in the twentieth century. Jesus Himself preached about the kingdom of God to large groups of five thousand to ten thousand people.

In the 1990s, thousands of men were motivated at huge Promise Keepers (PK) rallies held across the United States. Those who attended the Washington, D.C., rally in 1998 may remember how awesome it was to hear literally a million men praising God together.

Another advantage of the large-group dynamic is that it makes more room for diversity, which helps convey a sense of God's majesty and transcendence. Looking over the crowd at my first PK rally at Arrowhead Stadium in Kansas City, I noticed every shape, color, and culture sharing a unity and harmony (not musically) usually unique to large groups. What's more, a doctor sat on my right and a plumber flanked my left. Men in wheelchairs sat behind me and a senior citizen sat before me.

In general, people often sense a powerful movement of God's Spirit when believers unite in prayer and worship. And after the Friday evening service, one man shared that when he saw and heard thousands of men singing "How Great Thou Art" together, he started reconsidering the importance of God in his life, too.

Despite the advantages of inspiration, information, and momentum, the large-group dynamic also has limitations, as every pastor preparing for the Sunday morning message will confirm. Who, exactly, is the target audience? The mixed crowd includes so many people with varied backgrounds and needs that pastors may not know the key issues to address—much less how to communicate them effectively.

Another reality of the large-group dynamic is that few people can lead large groups well. Few possess the talent it takes to successfully minister to a large crowd. Those that do, make it look easy. When gifted Christian speakers like Bill Hybels or Rick Warren capture the attention of thousands, it's tempting to think, "I could do that!" I feel the same way watching Tiger Woods hit his tee shot. But, realistically, I can't begin to stir a crowd like they can or golf like Tiger.

When a ministry only values the large group dynamic, it creates frustrated, ineffective wannabes. Furthermore, when the only model of ministry is teaching and preaching before a crowd, most people get relegated to the sidelines and into the passive role of a spectator. That explains why Jesus didn't use the large-group dynamic as His main ministry model.

"It was in 323, almost three hundred years after the birth of the church, that Christians first met in something we now call a 'church building,'" writes James Rutz in *The Open Church*. "For all three hundred years before that, the church met in living rooms."![1] Indeed, during the first three centuries of church growth, leaders typically ministered without large-group dynamics. Persecution and the lack of megafacilities may partially explain why. However, when Christianity became a popular national religion under Roman emperor Constantine in the fourth century, large groups became the ministry norm.

Small ministries may create this dynamic by joining other churches for special worship celebrations, national conferences, and seminars. Big churches offer this dynamic every Sunday morning, which gives that group its own identity and momentum. However, the danger comes when a church devotes most of its energy and personnel to using the large-group driver and barely dusts off the rest of the clubs. In other words, when the large-group driver is the primary tool, it tends to become an end in itself rather than a means to effective discipleship. It can consume the energy of the whole community. And rather than contributing to the process of maturity, it just creates immature spectators. Rather than mobilizing the body to serve, it solidifies just a few to perform.

In stating the Great Commission, Jesus said that making disciples requires "teaching them to *observe* all that I commanded you" (Matthew 28:20, NASB; emphasis added). It is not just "teaching them all I have commanded you"! The important phrase "to observe" is critical to the disciplemaking process because it means following Jesus—not just listening

INTENTIONAL DISCIPLEMAKING

to His message. It's the difference between information and application.

According to research on American beliefs and practices, very little statistical difference exists between those who call themselves Christians and those who don't. Could it be that we are hitting long shots with the large-group dynamic, but landing in the woods with too little life-to-life putting?

At the end of Christ's Sermon on the Mount, He tells a parable about building a house (see Matthew 7:24-27). The difference between the house that stood and the house that fell was not information. They both were built with the same blueprint. The difference was in the foundations—sand versus rock, hearing versus doing.

A weakness of the large-group dynamic is the lack of solid personal application and accountability. Granted, some will take what they hear sitting in the pew and put it into practice outside the service. But for most, even good intentions get torpedoed when the service ends and real life explodes around the would-be disciple once again.

Small Groups: The Irons

Golfers use the irons to get the ball on or close to the green. Small groups work like these irons. Twenty years ago, churches using small groups were on the cutting edge of ministry. Today, churches not using small groups seem backward. Yet small groups only represent a means to an end: encouraging discipleship.

Small groups of four to twelve people typically move toward a more intimate community dynamic, one where members feel enough security and trust to share the dreams, fears, and concerns that they could never reveal in a larger group. Because it's harder to hide in a small group, a sense of ownership and responsibility to each other develops as well.

Wesley's Way
John Wesley depended on small groups in the eighteenth century after successfully preaching to crowds in the emerging

cities of Bristol and Kingswood, where the coal miners were especially responsive to the gospel. Though he preached to groups of five to six thousand in the early morning and up to twenty thousand in the evening, Wesley was not content with the large-group dynamic alone. He knew it would take something more intimate to disciple new Christians to spiritual maturity.

Ultimately, Wesley designed his Methodist movement with small groups to encourage maturity at every level. The resulting "classes," "bands," and "Select Societies" each focused on a different growth stage.[2] Classes invited seekers to explore and discover the reality of faith in Christ. Bands, on the other hand, gathered to encourage those already intent on building a holy life. According to Howard Snyder's book *The Radical Wesley*, band members would respond to questions such as (1) What known sins have you committed since our last meeting? (2) What temptations have you met with? (3) How were you delivered? and (4) What have you thought, said, or done of which you doubt whether it be sin or not?[3]

Finally, in addition to the various other leadership groups that developed around his lay preachers and pastors, Wesley also developed Select Societies, a complex, small-group matrix for personal holiness and discipleship among leaders.

Small-Group Strategies

There are two basic strategies for developing a small-group ministry today. The first involves forming a small group that grows toward spiritual maturity together over the long haul. One advantage is the intimacy that the group develops over time.

However, the weakness in this model becomes obvious when members inevitably mature at different rates. Even marriage partners rarely develop at the same pace. When this growth-rate disparity occurs, the stronger members—those striving for more commitment and discipling—can intimidate the others into following along. But those folks may inwardly be kicking and fighting to return to their previous comfort level. Eventually, the group will move on without the reluctant member(s), or it will stay stunted at the lowest common spiritual denominator.

Another weakness of this model involves the "empty chair" concept, which creates the expectation that new people will consistently join the group until it becomes large enough to divide. This creates tension because every group moves toward closure over time.

The terms "open" and "closed" in small-group language refer to a group's ability or desire to accept new members. Typically, if a small group becomes intimate, it closes. If it stays open in order to involve new members or expand, it fails to become intimate. Precious few small groups manage both intimacy and expansion.

The second small-group strategy uses a more academic model of progression. Each small group focuses on a particular need or stage of spiritual growth. Members move through the growth environments—from group to group—as they are able.

Under the leadership of its senior pastor, Tommy Nelson, Denton Bible Church in Denton, Texas, has developed a strong disciplemaking process facilitated by this type of fluid small-group system. Brad Davis, current director of the church's small-group ministry, explains that at Denton they organize these groups around the "Four Es of Maturity":

1. *Entering Stage:*
   Geographically organized care groups

2. *Establishing Stage:*
   Divorce recovery groups
   Parenting children groups
   Parenting teens groups
   Building a healthy marriage groups
   Preparing for marriage groups
   Men's and women's groups
   Financial stewardship groups

3. *Equipping Stage:*
   Discipleship training groups
   Evangelism training groups
   Lay Biblical Institute

4. *Employing Stage:*
   Missions groups
   Service groups
   Community projects groups
   Small-group leaders

When a member outgrows a small group, that person discusses the next step with his or her small-group leader. In this way, members can regularly assess their growth and prayerfully discern where to go to develop more. Incidentally, the equipping stage in this fluid model has helped the church train 95 percent of its leadership.

In an intentional disciplemaking community, every player knows where he or she fits in. When the big picture is understood, small-group leaders don't need to protect their turf or hoard their members. Rather, they send and receive people knowing that this method helps develop a kingdom-of-God citizen who is moving toward maturity.

Regardless of a small-group leader's strategy, the four critical elements within effective groups are care, growth, training, and task. These four elements closely parallel the spiritual growth process and, for that reason, every small group should offer them in varying degrees according to the group's focus. For instance, entry-level care or covenant groups will express a strong "care" orientation and a minimal "training and task" orientation. These groups will spend more time welcoming visitors and recruiting new members than serving in the food pantry or engaging in deep Bible studies.

On the other hand, a small group with a dominant training element may stick to a highly sequential spiritual education curriculum. Such a group will express the other elements, too, but to a lesser degree than its primary purpose. One winter, I regularly led a group like this. Though they were intent on discipleship training, when a couple in the group arrived with news that their unmarried daughter was pregnant, the training program went out the window when the group decided to focus instead on care and prayer.

The task of every new small group must be to decide which of the four elements will represent the group's focus. This is critical because nothing will frustrate members and leaders more than having different expectations.

Consider Bob. Bob attends a small group expecting it to be like the training-oriented group he was in last year. He anticipates growing through more Bible study, so he arrives motivated to do some serious digging in the Bible and expects everyone else to be similarly motivated.

Don, on the other hand, enters the group recovering from a sudden career change. He feels beaten up, ground up, and fed up. Emotionally spent and intellectually confused, Don wants to be involved in a care-oriented group. He's looking for someone to listen and to encourage him.

If carelessly placed in the same small group, Bob and Don could be on a collision course. Four weeks of getting to know the members in the group would be great for Don, but would totally aggravate Bob. The differing needs of Don and Bob underscore the importance of clarifying and communicating the structure of each small group to interested people.

The life span of each group needs to be defined as well. Some groups can accomplish their objectives in a few months while others will need to spend a few years together. On a subtler note, members should establish early on whether they want to be an open or closed group.

Each group also needs to identify the expected commitment level. Is the group a "come and go" group or one that demands regular attendance? Sometimes I ask members in the training groups I lead to sign a covenant agreement regarding expectations and objectives. In this way, I establish requirements that I hope will both test their resolve and help them finish strong.

Life to Life: The Putter

Of all the relational discipleship dynamics, the life-to-life dynamic remains the least understood, experienced, and practiced. Some ministry leaders have never been involved in a mentoring relationship. Therefore, they avoid using it in the discipleship process. For others, the life-to-life approach is too slow. They see an ocean of spiritually immature people, and the thought of meeting only one person at a time seems unproductive. Or perhaps they fear being accused of showing favoritism. Or it may seem emotionally safer to lead large meetings or small groups.

Serious golfers recognize the expression "Drive for show, putt for dough." No matter how good you look getting the ball to the green, if you can't putt it into the hole, you can't win. On the golf course, the putter gets used twice as much as any other club in the bag. Although it doesn't take great athletic ability to use a putter, using it well requires lots of practice.

When Jesus said, "[Teach] them to obey everything I have commanded you" (Matthew 28:20), He knew that application and accountability required plenty of individual connections. For instance, Jesus gave personal attention to people at all levels of the discipleship process—from the Samaritan woman at the well to Peter, whom He pulled aside after the Resurrection.

Dawson Trotman, founder of The Navigators, strongly believed in the need for this "man to man" or "woman to woman" approach. It was a central part of his strategy for reaching sailors during World War II. He spent time with them while they were in port and encouraged them to pass on what they had learned to others while they were at sea.

By the end of the war, thousands of men were using the man-to-man spiritual putter to reach their worlds for Christ. This strategy took The Navigators' ministry to college campuses after the war and, many spiritual generations later, reached me in the mid-1960s when I was a college student.

The spiritual putter goes by a variety of names. In

Connecting, authors Paul Stanley and Robert Clinton call it "mentoring," which they define as "a personal experience in which one person empowers another by sharing God-given resources."[4] They also identify a range of mentoring styles from the intensive to the occasional to the passive. Each situation demands its own style based on needs and resources.

In 2 Timothy 2:2, the apostle Paul shows how life-to-life relationships work in three directions. Paul mentored Timothy, and Timothy in turn mentored others. In addition, Timothy connected with "many witnesses"—evidently peers on the same spiritual journey—for sources of mutual encouragement, accountability, and protection.

As we age, mentoring can become an even more effective discipleship method. Howard and William Hendricks capture this idea in their book, *As Iron Sharpens Iron:* "Many men over age 55 are reaching for the bench, sliding for home. They are caving in at the very time when they ought to be tearing the place apart for Jesus Christ."[5] Mentoring, they note, is a great way to rejuvenate your passion for Christ and your sense of mission while encouraging someone else to grow in the same direction.

My eighty-two-year-old mother recently reflected on how difficult it had become for her to lead and participate in small-group Bible studies since her hearing began diminishing. "In a group, I have a hard time distinguishing sounds and hearing what people say," she explained. "But I can still do all right when it's just one other person. So I'm praying that God will give me one younger woman who I can invest in." My mother isn't planning on giving up on discipleship. She's just going to use her putter more.

CHAPTER SEVEN

Authentic
▌ Leadership

For Ezra had set his heart to study the law of the
Lord, and to practice it, and to teach His statutes
and ordinances in Israel.

Ezra 7:10 (NASB)

WHILE BROWSING AT Barnes and Noble the
other day, I was amazed at how many subjects had
"For Dummies" self-help books. *DOS for Dummies*, one of
the first "For Dummies" books published, appealed to computer illiterates. This user friendly series attempts to reduce
the complex to the simple for those who just need to get a
quick, practical grasp of a subject. So why couldn't I find a
"Leadership for Dummies" book on the shelves?

Leading an intentional disciplemaking community—be
it a large church or a small group—can be a very complex
undertaking. Why? It involves people—not just a program.
Can you guess which is tougher to understand?

Discipleship leadership is not a science, but an art of persuasion. For instance, a skilled discipleship leader can per-
suade others to understand a church building campaign as
more than just a brick-and-mortar project. The leader knows
how to communicate that the campaign is an opportunity to
build spiritual character in people as they sacrifice to complete

that new vision. In the same way, teaching people about conflict resolution can be a way not only to teach about peace, but also to develop peacemakers, forgivers, and humble servants.

This type of transformational leadership in an intentional disciplemaking community requires authenticity. A few years ago, Tommy Nelson, the pastor of Denton Bible Church mentioned in chapter 6, shared four questions at our Navigators staff conference that highlighted the critical role of authentic leadership in the intentional disciplemaking community:

- What kind of person is your community trying to produce?
- What kind of community produces that kind of person?
- What kind of leadership produces that kind of community?
- What kind of pastor produces that kind of leadership?

Three metaphors describe the kind of authentic leaders who drive intentional disciplemaking communities: model, coach, and parent. These metaphors show that it doesn't take spiritual gifting but spiritual maturity to become an authentic discipleship leader.

You may be a pastor, youth director, or superintendent. You may be a small-group leader, a board member, or have no title at all. Nevertheless, authentic transformational leadership is within reach if you follow the pattern of Ezra. First, he prepared his heart to seek God. Then, he applied what he learned. Finally, he passed that knowledge on to others. This process can be described in terms of a model, a coach, and a parent.

The Leader as a Model

Modeling authentic leadership creates an example for others to copy and then replicate. The clearer the model, the better the duplication potential. Leaders of intentional disciplemaking communities must be models, especially because the more complex a task is, the greater the need for a model.

During the holidays, my wife sets a jigsaw puzzle on a card table and recruits everyone to help her put it together. Jigsaw puzzles don't come with instructions, just a picture. When I attempt to participate in the project, I immediately understand the importance of the model picture. I can put those ten-piece kid's puzzles together without any help, but not the ten-thousand-piece ones Mary finds for Christmas. The box lid becomes our most valued tool. Woe to anyone who makes off with it.

Discipleship leaders constantly refer to Jesus in the same way my family refers to the box lid because He gives us the best picture of what God looks like. Remember that Jesus didn't just tell the apostles about God. He modeled God. Sure, there were the messages that attracted the crowds and con-fused the critics. But it was His life model that transformed them forever.

Others had great ethical messages that also drew crowds. Some of these teachers had high positions that gave them a hearing. But when Jesus spoke, His life—more than His words—opened eyes to truth. The truth in sandals changed the course of history.

In the classic book *The Master Plan of Evangelism*, Robert Coleman calls this ministry one of "association." He points out that as Jesus trained the disciples, "knowledge was gained by association before it was understood by explana-tion."[1] Jesus used no formal classroom, no lecture hall. His informal method contrasted with the formality of His day and ours. Then, when He had nearly completed training the twelve disciples, He announced His expectation: "And you will bear witness also, because you have been with Me from the beginning" (John 15:27, NASB).

"*Listen* to me and I will make you fishers of men" is how many tend to interpret those words—with the emphasis on "listen." Some leaders believe that if they can package the Christian message just right and sell it with enthusiasm, people will follow. But plenty of pastors and church leaders feel frustrated after years of telling people what they should do and how to do it without creating many new followers of Jesus.

In 1968, "Follow Me" was the motto on my unit patch in Infantry Officer Candidate School at Fort Bragg, an army base in North Carolina. The words surrounded a vertical sword and symbolized what we would become—leaders. In six short months, we would be transformed from privates into lieutenants. The initial weeks of the officer-training course flew by. The learning curve was steep, though, and we were too intimidated to think rationally.

Then one day it dawned on some of us that this was not just a training exercise; this was for real! There was a war going on in Southeast Asia that would more than likely become our first tour. The U.S. Army needed second lieutenant infantry officers because our predecessors were getting shot at a very high rate. Suddenly, "Follow Me" didn't look so good. So we came up with the substitute slogan: "Quit Pushing!"

Some things can be taught verbally and acquired conceptually. But flying an airplane and disciplemaking are not among them. I would not knowingly step aboard an aircraft piloted by someone who had just learned to fly by attending lectures or studying Microsoft's Flight Simulator 98 manual. Yet some church leaders ask their congregations to step into a similar situation every day. For instance, when I spoke with Bill, the pastor of a growing church in Kansas City, he wanted to learn more about intentional disciplemaking. We talked about the need for establishing a clear picture of the end result as well as the importance of developing leaders in his church who could model disciplemaking to others.

"This is where we have a problem," Bill confessed. "I have been trained in how to study the Bible, in how to preach, and even in how to manage a church. But I have never been trained in how to make disciples. I've never seen anyone do it, let alone having done it." Bill had caught the vision of discipleship and had the heart to make disciples, but struggled for lack of a model.

King David modeled leadership when he followed Saul

as king of the developing nation of Israel. Under this leadership, Israel grew from a network of families to a strong national power during the successive reigns of Saul, David, and Solomon.

Yet Israel got off to a shaky start. Saul had been selected king, but king of what? There was little cohesiveness, little momentum, and few resources. When the Philistines attacked Israel's army under King Saul, valiant warriors were hard to come by. When the giant Goliath challenged the army, only one giant killer could be found—David, an adolescent shepherd.

Yet when David became king, he trained thirty mighty men as giant killers. He kept sixteen others in reserve to fill the coveted spots on the giant-killer team. Why did David have a surplus and Saul a deficit? Well, David was a giant killer and Saul was not. David needed no messages, no threats, no manipulation, no bribes. Just a simple "Follow me" worked for Jesus and David.

However, it's easy for church leaders to hide behind pulpits, desks, and titles instead of modeling Christ. Why? Because modeling requires authenticity. It requires practicing what you preach and teach, which benefits both the model and the observer. Opening your life to intimate observation can actually be quite healthy.

A few years ago, I started a small group with three men who wanted to develop a devotional life and memorize Scripture. We met once a week at 6 A.M. I knew I could teach discipleship skills; I had done it hundreds of times. But now I was vulnerable. I couldn't rely on last year's success or a nice handout.

Leading by modeling helped me practice what I was teaching. I was motivated to a higher standard because of the accountability of this group. Had I given a workshop on the subject, I could have hidden behind the overhead and never been challenged myself.

Paul's letters to Timothy testify to the power of one person modeling Christian faith to another because what Paul taught, he lived. Timothy keenly observed his mentor, which gave Paul the confidence to tell him, "You, however, know all about my teaching, my way of life, my purpose, faith, patience, love, endurance, persecutions, sufferings. . . . But as for you, continue in what you have learned and have become convinced of" (2 Timothy 3:10,14). Ultimately, Paul challenges Timothy to model Christian faith for others.

Duane was the first Navigator I met while in college. He led our campus ministry, and I was curious about Duane's teaching on discipleship during our weekly meetings. But those messages have long left my memory bank. No matter. His biggest influence on my understanding of this topic took place when he invited me to spend a weekend with him and his family. During those three days, I still remember watching him handle each situation with grace and wisdom. I saw discipleship in action, an authentic leader who modeled what I wanted to be.

The Leader as a Coach

In some respects, modeling leadership seems passive when compared to coaching leadership. A coach models but also explains the whys and hows of discipleship. Seeing others acquiring the skills and abilities to perform well motivates a coach. And he or she only succeeds when the players succeed. Furthermore, coaching involves developing individuals and building a team.

In *Connecting,* authors Paul Stanley and J. Robert Clinton define coaching as "a relational process in which a mentor, who knows how to do something well, imparts those skills to a mentoree who wants to learn them."[2] Later in the book they write, "Coaching is a process of imparting encouragement and skills to succeed in a task through a relationship."[3]

Good coaches may say, "You're doing it wrong," but they add, "and here is what you need to do it right." Coaches believe in potential. The possibility of future successes motivates them.

Coaching happens in all areas of life—sports, music, education, business, and more—even though a different term may be used to describe it. For the intentional disciplemaking leader, good coaching involves mastery of five key areas: communication, concentration, demonstration, evaluation, and correlation.

Communication

More than once, I have read a book on an exciting subject and floundered when I tried to explain the key ideas to someone else. Usually, I embarrass myself with stuttering before I finally suggest that the listener "read the book." Had I reached a deeper level of understanding, I could have better shared what I had read.

Coaches, on the other hand, know their "game" well enough to explain it to others. Their subject is their specialty. It is like a thread that runs through their whole life. They read about it, think about it, and are drawn to others with the same life thread.

Paul's letters to Timothy have great examples of effective coaching communication. Paul not only models how to develop disciplemaking communities, but also explains the process clearly. Consider this sample of his coaching pointers:

- Kindle afresh the gift of God, which is in you. (2 Timothy 1:6, NASB)
- Retain the standard of sound words, which you have heard from me. (2 Timothy 1:13, NASB)
- Guard, through the Holy Spirit who dwells in us, the treasure which has been entrusted to you. (2 Timothy 1:14, NASB)
- Be strong in the grace that is in Christ Jesus. (2 Timothy 2:1)
- And the things which you have heard from me . . . entrust to faithful men. (2 Timothy 2:2, NASB)
- Suffer hardship with me, as a good soldier of Christ Jesus. (2 Timothy 2:3, NASB)
- Remember Jesus Christ. (2 Timothy 2:8)

Timothy had heard these instructions before. They had been the focus of many late-evening meetings and early-morning discussions. And Paul had discussed them in town after town, so Timothy heard them over and over. Still, Paul continued challenging Timothy to understand them well enough to effectively share them with someone else (see 2 Timothy 2:2).

Concentration

During the 1960s, legendary Green Bay Packer coach Vince Lombardi was said to begin the practice season by holding up a football and declaring, "Gentlemen, this is a football." Lombardi ruthlessly concentrated on the fundamentals of football—regardless of whether he stood before rookies or before seasoned players.

Coach John Wooden, who retired with ten NCAA basketball championships, was a coach's coach. In his book *They Call Me Coach,* he describes his philosophy of coaching success:

> It isn't what you do, but how you do it. No system
> is any good if the players are not well grounded in
> fundamentals. Team play comes from integrating
> individuals who have mastered the fundamentals
> into a smooth working unit. Confidence comes
> from being prepared.[4]

Like these outstanding athletic coaches, effective disciplemaking leaders concentrate on the fundamentals of how to "know Christ and make Him known." Popular new waves of interest will sweep over the church—trends and hot issues that seem important. But the disciplemaking coach must stick to the fundamentals of spiritual conditioning, ministry skills, and teamwork.

In making disciples, I have learned never to assume that the fundamentals are in place. Instead, I review them with The Navigators' "wheel" illustration of Christian faith. Christ occupies the hub of this wheel. The rim represents the obedient Christian life, and the four spokes that hold the wheel together

INTENTIONAL DISCIPLEMAKING

are the Word, prayer, fellowship, and witnessing. This illustration of these six fundamentals has been used all over the world to establish a solid framework for spiritual maturity.

Demonstration

Early in my spiritual journey, my mentors encouraged me to read the stories of men and women of faith who were historic models of disciplemaking. Corrie ten Boom, Jim Elliot, Charles Spurgeon, C. T. Studd, William Carey, Hudson Taylor, and Dietrich Bonhoeffer stood out. But one of my most profound models came from a small pamphlet entitled *George Mueller: Man of Faith*.

The short testimony of the nineteenth-century, British-born Mueller made an indelible mark on me. Though he lived in a completely different era, his confident belief in God's provision prompted me to start stepping out of my comfort zone, out of my limited resources, and out of my engineering career to become involved in a full-time ministry.

God provides models in every generation, and wise coaches point out those models. A wise coach doesn't feel threatened by others who do it better, but welcomes the chance to promote quality demonstrations in a variety of uniforms.

Evaluation

Years ago, Lorne Sanny, then president of The Navigators, often reminded us that staff typically want to ask three questions of their supervisor:

- What is expected of me?
- How am I doing?
- Will you help me when I need it?

During my first assignment, building a disciplemaking community among students at St. Cloud State College in St. Cloud, Minnesota, I faced a huge adjustment. I had just returned from military duty and had never worked on staff with The Navigators before. During those initial three years,

I was motivated, intense, and proactive—and also a little paranoid. Why? Because I wasn't sure what to do, how to do it, or how well it was being done.

Periodically, my wife and I received visits from others higher on The Navigators totem pole. We had great visits, and they contributed to our ministry. But I never knew how they evaluated our work.

The Navigators next assigned us to Illinois State University in Bloomington. Alan Andrews, currently the U.S. director for The Navigators, was my supervisor and coach there. Thanks to Alan's regular evaluations, I developed into a more confident player. For instance, he helped me clarify the elements of a disciplemaking community, helped me evaluate the success of my ministry, and gave me resources when I needed them. Because he had learned how to competently evaluate, correct, and instruct, I grew confident enough to continue in my ministry—something I've done for the past thirty years.

Disciplemaking leaders willingly assess and correct. They don't judge, but honestly try to support growth in those they coach. They avoid trying to impress people with what they know or what they have done. Instead, they focus on developing others to their fullest potential. They also realize that it's not only what you say but also how you say it that influences others. Finally, they don't treat everyone in the same way—they remain sensitive to God as they help build spiritual maturity in the lives of others.

Correlation

Usually, coaching involves not only developing individuals, but also developing teams. The same is true in disciplemaking. Disciples are not developed in isolation, but rather in the context of community, so leaders need to develop a team to carry out the disciplemaking process. One person cannot do it all alone.

In the disciplemaking ministries I lead, we usually define the process in four stages: evangelizing, establishing, equipping, and empowering. However, as people develop in their ministry skills, they each contribute best in one or two of the stages. It's not that they couldn't contribute in all four, but each most definitely exhibits a bent toward certain ones. My job then involves finding that correlation and developing it.

In one church, we established groups for each stage of growth. During that first year, we placed our leaders in groups without making a correlation with *their* ministry bent. For instance, one dynamic couple led one of our entry-level care groups. Don and Lora were willing, and we had a need. But their hearts were much more geared for the equipping phase. The result of this mismatch? They felt frustrated on the low commitment of group members, and group members felt frustrated on the high expectations this couple kept projecting. The next year, when we placed leaders according to their strengths, we got much better small-group dynamics.

So a wise coach helps the players discover their best fit and play their position. Denny Crum, head basketball coach at the University of Louisville in Kentucky, both played and coached alongside Wooden. In the foreword of Wooden's book *They Call Me Coach*, Crum wrote about the impact Wooden had on him and others:

> He's touched the lives of those around him and inspired countless people to emulate his wonderful qualities: his love and dedication to his family, his appreciation of all who played for him, his honesty, his patience, and his modesty. He could teach, imparting his thoughts in a way that never alienated anyone, and he could understand the frustration of a player who wanted to play better so badly he could taste it. He controlled the most stressful situation, with the ease and demeanor of a gentleman, and, most important, he knew how to listen.
>
> It still amazes me how much a coach rubs off on you. . . . Whenever I speak publicly, which is often, I credit John Wooden for the success we've had here at Louisville. Most of what I know about basketball I learned at his side.[5]

The Leader as a Parent

Just as a coach is more than a model, a parent is more than a coach. The parental style of leadership adds two additional dynamics—grace and an ongoing sense of spiritual family lineage.

In the Old Testament, Jewish parents discipled their children to ensure that the next generation would follow God. Fathers in particular were to instruct, teach, and develop their children. This classic Old Testament passage to Israel spells it out clearly:

> Love the LORD your God with all your heart and with all your soul and with all your strength. These commandments that I give you today are to be upon your hearts. Impress them on your children. Talk about them when you sit at home and when you walk along the road, when you lie down and when you get up. Tie them as symbols on your hands and bind them on your foreheads. Write them on the doorframes of your houses and on your gates. (Deuteronomy 6:5-9)

So, besides modeling God's truth, the parent would diligently pass it on to the next generation. This discipling process was not a once-a-week Sabbath lecture or a job for the Jewish Education Department. It was a parental responsibility that covered all of life—sitting, walking, sleeping, and waking. Had Moses written this today, he would have included "driving to soccer practice."

The apostle Paul encourages disciplemaking with the parent metaphor as well:

> Even though you have ten thousand guardians in Christ, you do not have many fathers, for in Christ Jesus I became your father through the gospel. (1 Corinthians 4:15)

But we were gentle among you, like a mother caring
for her little children. We loved you so much that
we were delighted to share with you not only the
gospel of God but our lives as well, because you
had become so dear to us. Surely you remember,
brothers, our toil and hardship; we worked night
and day in order not to be a burden to anyone while
we preached the gospel of God to you.

You are witnesses, and so is God, of how holy,
righteous and blameless we were among you who
believed. For you know that we dealt with each
of you as a father deals with his own children,
encouraging, comforting and urging you to live
lives worthy of God. (1 Thessalonians 2:7-12)

More than modeling or coaching, parenting emphasizes
grace in the disciplemaking process with images of a mother's
tender touch as well as a father's persistent encouragement.
And that's a good thing.

Karen grew up without a dad. Raised by a demanding
mother, she found identity in athletics—identity, but no
security. And though she accepted Christ as a college student, those deep-seated insecurities affected her relationship
with God.

One day, she confided that much of her Christian devo-
tion stemmed from her fears and insecurities, rather than
from a love for God. That's why disciplemaking communities
need to emphasize that grace is at the heart of the Christian
family. Sure, this community expects spiritual growth. But
leaders must highlight the accepting nature of God's grace,
which says, "No matter what, I will still love you."

John records this kind of loving grace during the final
Passover Jesus spent with His disciples: "Having loved His
own who were in the world, He loved them to the end" (John
13:1, NASB). Just after this statement, John writes that Judas
leaves the meal and plots the final steps of his betrayal. He
leads the guards to the Garden of Gethsemane later that night
to hand Christ over to the authorities. I'm sure that as he

approaches Jesus, the Leader who loved to the end, he is shocked. Why? Because Jesus greets him not as an adversary, not by a rebuke, but with the word "friend" (Matthew 26:50).

Authentic disciplemaking leaders must clearly communicate that grace is not only accepting; it also never gives up. Down is not out, failure is not final, and there is always tomorrow. People may disappoint us. They may refuse to move toward maturity. They may even challenge our motives. But because of God's grace, we can always offer hope.

CHAPTER EIGHT

Ministering Beyond Your Means

But we have this treasure in jars of clay to show that this all-surpassing power is from God and not from us.

2 Corinthians 4:7

SUCCESSFULLY LEADING AN intentional disciple-making community reminds me of successfully sailing a boat. A captain understands that a sailboat has no power of its own. Rather, it moves only if someone hoists up the sails and positions them to best catch the wind—the real power source. On some sailboats, captains may use a small outboard motor to get in and out of ports. But without the sails up to catch the wind, it's impossible to make real progress.

Disciplemaking leaders must understand that only the wind of God's Spirit can move an individual to a transformed, spiritually mature life. Without recognizing this, a leader will float on the water, powerless to do much more than inefficiently paddle for progress. However, by raising spiritual sails and learning navigational skills, that same leader—one so limited by human efforts—can minister beyond his or her means. An exhilarating journey lies ahead for those who can sail out of port into the open sea.

Unfortunately, the Old Testament is littered with the shipwrecked examples of those who failed to learn spiritual sailing skills. The kings of Israel repeatedly began their leadership depending on God. But after achieving some success, they reverted to reliance on other things.

To avoid being spiritually stranded or shipwrecked, disciplemaking leaders need to hoist and skillfully wield four sails. Other sails exist, but main mast sails for effective ministry include prayer, brokenness, faith, and intimacy.

The Sail of Prayer

Before skipping over this section with an indignant thought—"Duh. Everyone knows that!"—consider these oft-underestimated aspects of prayer that, when developed, help this sail unfold.

Praise

God designed humans to worship. In Romans 1:21-23, Paul explains that you will either worship the invisible Creator God or something less (yourself, nature, money, and so on), but you will worship. So directing all your worship, your praise, toward God is a critical part of effective disciplemaking. In addition, praise involves thanksgiving. Regularly thank God for what you know is true about His character as well as for what He has done and what He will do.

There are two times when praise is critical—when we feel like it and when we don't! During a particularly stressful period in my ministry, Ruth Myer's little book *31 Days of Praise* (Multnomah, 1998) encouraged me to lift this sail higher when it could have crumpled into a heap on the deck of my life. In these pages, I found her to be an inspiring mentor. Her words helped me articulate my praise during that difficult time. And as I focused on God's character and praised Him, I found the power to hoist the prayer sail up— even though I felt weak with discouragement.

Remember that almost every major prayer recorded in

Scripture begins with praise or thanksgiving. The Psalms overflow with praises that moved the psalmists out of discouragement, despair, or defeat to a new hope. Praise releases spiritual adrenalin, which will help you hoist that sail morning after morning. It's like a cup of coffee at 6 A.M. When you praise God, you will get new perspective, new energy, and renewed hope.

David points out in Psalm 22:3 that God's Spirit rides on the praises of His people. King Jehoshaphat provides a vivid picture of this truth. This Old Testament king believed God when He promised to deliver Israel from the overwhelming armies of Ammon and Moab. So Jehoshaphat's battle strategy involved putting the praise band in front of his army, and they marched into battle to get the victory: "As they began to sing and praise, the LORD set ambushes against the men of Ammon and Moab and Mount Seir who were invading Judah, and they were defeated" (2 Chronicles 20:22).

Promises

While vacationing in Washington state, our family set aside one day to drive up Hurricane Ridge and view majestic Mount Olympus. After that day, we needed to travel out of the region. Not surprisingly, it had rained on the previous days and the day of our ascent began in the same way. We debated whether the drive would be worth it. Because it was rainy and cloudy at sea level, how could we hope for blue skies at five thousand feet?

We decided to go, nonetheless. Several times, as the fog thickened, I threatened to turn around. But as we passed the five-thousand-foot mark, the clouds miraculously cleared and we viewed the most breathtaking scene of our vacation thus far. The jagged Olympic Range peaks jutted up into the sunshine and created a vivid relief against the dark clouds below. I felt embarrassed that I had questioned the worth of the trip.

Later I reflected on how much more enjoyable the journey up the mountain would have been had I asked the ranger at the base about the weather at the top. He would have told me that the top was clear, and to enjoy the trip. God's promises tell us the same thing—what it's really like beyond the rain and fog. He knows, and His promises encourage us to believe Him and press on.

His divine power has given us everything we need
for life and godliness through our knowledge of
him who called us by his own glory and goodness.
Through these he has given us his very great and
precious promises, so that through them you may
participate in the divine nature and escape the cor-
ruption in the world caused by evil desires.
(2 Peter 1:3-4)

Peter explains that believing in God's promises leads toward spiritual maturity because it involves partaking more closely in God's divine nature. By studying God's promises, you can see what's on God's heart and, ultimately, what His will is. By lifting this sail in your disciplemaking ministry, you can partner more closely with God's Spirit to accomplish His plan. Rather than praying to convince God to bless your plans, trust that God's promises will guide you into living by His plans.

God's promises need to be claimed, but most involve meeting conditions. God gives them and then waits for His people to step up and receive them. For instance, when our son was about six years old, he inherited his sister's training bike. Our family lives by the motto of using things until they wear out or break, and this bike had more miles left. After inheriting the hand-me-down, he quietly asked me if he could have his own bike.

"Dad," he began, "this bike is pink and has white tires on it. I want a real boy's bike—one that's black with knobby tires." I heard him, and decided to make a promise: if he would learn to ride his sister's training bike, I would get him his own black one with dirt-kicking tires.

He practiced and by spring took off the training wheels. Then one day he came to claim his promise. Of course, I gave him the meanest-looking black bike I could find. I had the resources all along, but I wanted to see if my son really wanted that bike. All he had to do was meet the condition and ask.

I think that in some small way, God operates like that. He doesn't hold out on fulfilling promises because He lacks the resources or only reluctantly gives gifts. Rather, He waits to see if we remember His promises and return to claim them.

King David intensely wanted to build a house for God. The prophet Nathan tells David that God will build a house for him and that, ultimately, one of David's sons will build the house for God.

David responds by humbling himself before God, by praying to claim the promise, and by storing resources. He prayed that God would simply fulfill His promise:

> And now, LORD, let the promise you have made concerning your servant and his house be established forever. Do as you promised, . . . O LORD, you are God! You have promised these good things to your servant. (1 Chronicles 17:23,26)

Sure enough, years later David's son Solomon built God's house and dedicated it by acknowledging the promise God made to his father, David:

> Praise be to the LORD, the God of Israel, who with his hands has fulfilled what he promised with his mouth to my father David. . . . I have succeeded David my father and . . . I have built the temple for the Name of the LORD, the God of Israel. . . . And now, O LORD, God of Israel, let your word that you promised your servant David come true. (2 Chronicles 6:4,10,17)

Solomon continues to build on that promise as he looks to the future and prays, asking God to carry out what had been promised.

Nehemiah also prayed with an eye on God's promises. For instance, before he approached the king, he reviewed the promise God made to both scatter and gather his people (see Nehemiah 1:5-11). They had been scattered, but now Nehemiah sought to reestablish Jerusalem. His confidence in God's promise fortified him enough to face the opposition ahead.

The first promise I ever claimed from God was the one for eternal life found in John 3:16. Though centuries old, it became a new promise for me when I claimed it for myself. However, during my ensuing journey with Christ, I have discovered many other promises God made and wants me to claim.

Are your life and ministry built on the promises of God? Is your confidence in what God sees or in what you can see? When the fog is the thickest, God's promises are the brightest. That's why this sail must be lifted day after day.

"Parental" Petitions

In an intentional disciplemaking community, prayer needs to focus on transformation. In Matthew 6:9-13, Jesus teaches the disciples how to pray by praying seven elements that shape a basic prayer. Then in John 17, He models a prayer for a discipler—a spiritual parent. As Jesus prays, He clarifies what is important to God, what is important in the life of disciples, and what must be accomplished through prayer. He also underscores the importance of five other areas:

1. Unity (verse 11)
2. Protection (verse 15)
3. Transformation (verse 17)
4. Spiritual generations (verses 20-21)
5. Intimacy (verse 24)

All these characteristics give a disciplemaking leader a solid prayer framework. Praying for these things not only calls on the Spirit of God, but also exercises our own disciplemaking efforts. Praying along these lines causes disciplers to focus on what's in God's heart regarding spiritual maturity.

The apostle Paul offers other prayer patterns helpful in guiding the disciplemaker's prayer life. In the following passages, note not only what Paul prays for, but also what he neglects to mention. How do your parental petitions for the lost or spiritually immature compare with his? Do you raise this section of the prayer sail daily?

> I keep asking that the God of our Lord Jesus Christ, the glorious Father, may give you the Spirit of wisdom and revelation, so that you may know him better. I pray also that the eyes of your heart may be enlightened in order that you may know the hope to which he has called you. (Ephesians 1:17-18)

> That . . . he may strengthen you with power through his Spirit in your inner being, . . . that you, being rooted and established in love, may have power . . . to grasp how wide and long and high and deep is the love of Christ, and to know this love that surpasses knowledge. (Ephesians 3:16-19)

> And this is my prayer: that your love may abound more and more in knowledge and depth of insight. (Philippians 1:9)

> We have not stopped praying for you and asking God to fill you with the knowledge of his will through all spiritual wisdom and understanding. (Colossians 1:9)

The Sail of Brokenness

King David wrote, "The sacrifices of God are a broken spirit; a broken and contrite heart, O God, you will not despise" (Psalm 51:17). The brokenness of dying a spiritual death to sin—particularly the sin of pride—opens another important sail. Jesus uses this concept of brokenness when He says, "I tell you the truth, unless a kernel of wheat falls to the ground and dies, it remains only a single seed. But if it dies, it produces many seeds" (John 12:24).

Brokenness doesn't refer to somebody who is cracked into a million pieces. Rather, it describes someone humbled from the way God has wrought correction or change through circumstances or discipline. The writer of Hebrews knew that, while often uncomfortable, the process of being broken—humbled—is extremely valuable (see Hebrews 12:11). But God's discipline alone will not produce the kind of brokenness necessary for effective disciplemaking. It depends on your response, too. Some rebel against God; others transform into a person more like Jesus.

For instance, Paul humbled himself as he chose to count all things as less than nothing in his desire to know Christ (see Philippians 3:8) and when he gave up his rights in order to serve others (see 1 Corinthians 9).

In the Old Testament, Israel's broken kings succeeded and were powerful. On the other hand, proud, self-sufficient kings turned out to be failures. Consider these examples:

- King Uzziah: "But after Uzziah became powerful, his pride led to his downfall. He was unfaithful to the LORD his God." (2 Chronicles 26:16)
- King Asa: "Then Asa called to the LORD his God and said, 'LORD, there is no one like you to help the powerless against the mighty. Help us, O LORD our God, for we rely on you, and in your name we have come against this vast army.'" (2 Chronicles 14:11)

Asa's prayer sounds impressive, but a few years later this proud king makes an alliance with the king of Aram. A prophet then announces God's judgment against Asa and prefaces it by saying, "For the eyes of the LORD range throughout the earth to strengthen those whose hearts are fully committed to him" (2 Chronicles 16:9).

Brokenness happens when you realize that you are a channel rather than a source; that you are dependent rather than independent. Brokenness means performing for an audience of One.

INTENTIONAL DISCIPLEMAKING

Years ago, my daughter performed as a violinist in the Missouri State Orchestra. Students from across the state were selected for this four-day event, which included a guest conductor from a major university. After the orchestra's grand performance, I asked her for whom she played— whom she sought to please. She thought for a minute before replying, "My only concern was whether the conductor thought we did a good job. During the performance, I wasn't even conscious of the audience."

Ultimately, brokenness means surrendering to the will of God—a sure sign of spiritual maturity. Even Jesus struggled to follow God's will, as revealed in the Garden of Gethsemane. Like Him, you may be tempted to escape the will of God. However, in escaping, you can miss seeing God's power billowing your sails and moving you closer to ministry victories.

The Sail of Faith

After spending forty years in blowing sand, the children of Israel found themselves on the edge of a swollen Jordan River during the flood season. They had no bridges, no ferries, no boats or barges. To enter the Promised Land, they had to accomplish the impossible.

"No way, Joshua," they must have grumbled. "Your leadership is questionable and your judgments are suspect. Nice timing!"

Imagine you're one of the priests assigned to carry the ark of the covenant. Joshua obviously believes God and tells you and the others to grab the ark and start walking into the water. You take a quick glance over your shoulder and see the entire nation. Your close friends stare, jaws dropped. Will you look stupid and foolish? Will God actually meet you with power? He did it years ago at the Red Sea, but what about now? What about for this generation? Where is Moses when you need him?

As soon as the priests who carried the ark reached the Jordan and their feet touched the water's edge, the water from upstream stopped flowing. It piled up in a heap a great distance away, at a town called Adam. (Joshua 3:15-16)

This story illustrates two principles of faith. The first is that *acting* on faith releases God's power. As long as they stood on the bank, there would be no power, no miracle, no dry land—no Promised Land. Faith expressed in obedience resulted in God exerting His power on their behalf.

The second is that acting on faith doesn't necessarily produce apparent results. Faith and obedience can still result in wet feet when God's power is not immediately revealed. After all, the priests' miracle happened upstream—well out of sight—as they stood in the mud and rushing water with a nation watching. To catch God's power, they had to keep the sail of faith up for a long time—as might you.

The Sail of Intimacy

For many of us "intimate" is an intimidating word. Wives say they want it, and husbands are not sure what it is. The dictionary defines "intimate" as "pertaining to the inmost character of a thing, essential; most private or personal; closely associated, very familiar" (*Webster's New World Dictionary*, 2nd ed.).

To know and be known at the center of our being is intimacy—something that is most fulfilled in relationship with Christ. The apostle Paul addresses intimacy with God when he writes to the Philippians, "I want to know Christ and the power of his resurrection and the fellowship of sharing in his sufferings, becoming like him in his death" (Philippians 3:10). From Paul's perspective, knowing Christ was not an intellectual or doctrinal pursuit alone. It was relational, experiential.

Jesus describes this intimate connection with a grapevine metaphor: "I am the vine; you are the branches. If a man remains in me and I in him, he will bear much fruit; apart from me you can do nothing" (John 15:5). Without lifting

INTENTIONAL DISCIPLEMAKING

the sail of intimacy with Christ, you'll have nothing—no life, no fruit, no power.

In his book *In the Name of Jesus*, Henri Nouwen wrote,

> The central question is, "Are the leaders of the future truly men and women of God, people with an ardent desire to dwell in God's presence, to listen to God's voice, to look at God's beauty, to touch God's incarnate Word and to taste fully God's infinite goodness?"[1]

In other words, beware that your compelling ministry vision would replace your passion for intimacy with Christ. Don't let toiling for Him become more exciting than walking with Him and don't let serving the King supersede knowing the King.

King David, great ruler and warrior that he was, stayed centered on knowing God: "Better is one day in your courts than a thousand elsewhere" (Psalm 84:10). Other verses speak of this intimacy as well, including Psalm 27:4: "One thing I ask of the LORD, this is what I seek: that I may dwell in the house of the LORD all the days of my life, to gaze upon the beauty of the LORD and to seek him in his temple."

Intimacy with Christ involves vulnerability, priority, and consistency—it is never gained where exposure is limited. Holding back from allowing Christ to touch every area of your life keeps Him at a distance, and you will suffer spiritually for this gap.

However, if you and your disciplemaking community hoist the sail of intimacy high, you will notice the spiritual breeze picking up. And with all the sails open, you will one day enter the harbor of heaven with plenty of company to see God most intimately—face to face.

Notes

Chapter 1: Arrested Spiritual Development?

1. Richard Foster, *Celebration of Discipline* (New York: HarperCollins, 1978), p. 1.
2. Gene Getz, *Sharpening the Focus of the Church* (Chicago: Moody, 1974), p. 53. See also Jim Petersen, *Lifestyle Discipleship* (Colorado Springs, Colo.: NavPress, 1993), chapter 3.

Chapter 2: Discipleship Blueprints

1. From a joint statement on discipleship, Eastbourne Consultation, September 24, 1999, Eastbourne, England.

Chapter 3: Transformation Versus Conformation

1. Os Guiness, *The Call* (Nashville, Tenn.: Word, 1998), p. 85.
2. Edwin Abbott, *Flatland: A Parable of Many Dimensions* (New York: Penguin, 1984).
3. Dallas Willard, *The Divine Conspiracy* (New York: HarperCollins, 1998), p. 58.

Chapter 4: Evangelism Unpacked

1. George Barna, *Evangelism That Works* (Ventura, Calif.: Regal, 1995), p. 84.
2. Jan Hettinga, *Follow Me* (Colorado Springs, Colo.: NavPress, 1996).
3. Barna found that only 12 percent of those that do evangelism feel they have a gift for it (see *Evangelism That Works*, p. 73).
4. Lee Strobel, *Inside the Mind of Unchurched Harry and Mary* (Grand Rapids, Mich.: Zondervan, 1993).

5. George Barna, *The Frog in the Kettle* (Ventura, Calif.: Regal, 1990).
6. Barna, *Evangelism That Works*, p. 38.
7. Jim Petersen, *Church Without Walls* (Colorado Springs, Colo.: NavPress, 1992), p. 118.
8. James Rutz, *The Open Church* (Auburn, Maine: The SeedSowers, 1992), p. 55.

Chapter 5: Overcoming Barriers
1. Michael Green, *Evangelism Through the Local Church* (Nashville, Tenn.: Nelson, 1990), p. 224.
2. Steve Sjogren, *Conspiracy of Kindness* (Ann Arbor, Mich.: Vine Books, 1993).
3. Bob and Betty Jacks, *Your Home a Lighthouse* (Colorado Springs, Colo.: NavPress, 1986).

Chapter 6: Discipleship Dynamics
1. James Rutz, *The Open Church* (Auburn, Maine: The SeedSower, 1992), p. 47.
2. Howard Snyder, *The Radical Wesley* (Downers Grove, Ill.: InterVarsity, 1980), p. 61.
3. Snyder, p. 60.
4. Paul Stanley and J. Robert Clinton, *Connecting* (Colorado Springs, Colo.: NavPress, 1992), p. 38.
5. Howard and William Hendricks, *As Iron Sharpens Iron* (Chicago: Moody, 1995), p. 149.

Chapter 7: Authentic Leadership
1. Robert Coleman, *The Master Plan of Evangelism* (Grand Rapids, Mich.: Revell, 1996), p. 39.
2. Paul Stanley and J. Robert Clinton, *Connecting* (Colorado Springs, Colo.: NavPress, 1992), p. 79.
3. Stanley and Clinton, p. 76.
4. John Wooden, *They Call Me Coach* (Chicago: Contemporary Books, 1988), p. 95.
5. Wooden, p. 7.

Chapter 8: Ministering Beyond Your Means
1. Henri Nouwen, *In the Name of Jesus* (New York: Crossroad, 1990), p. 30.

About the
Author

RON BENNETT grew up in Iowa where he graduated from Iowa State University with a bachelor's of science degree in aerospace engineering. While in college he met The Navigators and developed a heart and vision for discipleship.

After serving as an officer in the U.S. Army and completing a tour of duty in Vietnam, Ron joined the staff of The Navigators. As field staff, he has led ministries on campuses, in the military, and in the community. Along with directing field ministries, Ron has served as interim pastor for a local church.

Ron, his wife, Mary, and their four children make their home in the Kansas City area where he serves as a coach and consultant with churches and ministry leaders. Ron currently serves on the National Leadership Team of the Church Discipleship Ministry of The Navigators. He has been serving with The Navigators since 1970.

253
B4724
101643

PRACTICAL DISCIPLESHIP FOR EVERYDAY BELIEVERS.

Side by Side

Helping people move closer to Christ brings joy—but also some study and preparation. Whether you're a pastor, small-group leader, Sunday school teacher, one-on-one mentor, or just interested in developing your own faith, *Side by Side* will guide you through the lifelong process of discipleship.
Side by Side (Steve Rabey and Lois Mowday Rabey) $24.99

The River Within

Do you feel burned out or bored when it comes to your Christian walk? *The River Within* will open your eyes to a new way of living that brings you closer to God and plunges you into the passionate joy of living.
The River Within (Jeff Imbach) $15

Daily Discipleship

Filled with real-life stories, *Daily Discipleship* offers practical and encouraging teaching on what it means to be a disciple who follows Jesus in the midst of living a busy and full life.
Daily Discipleship (LeRoy Eims) $13

Get your copies today at your local bookstore, visit our website at www.navpress.com, or call (800) 366-7788 and ask for offer **#6144** or a FREE catalog of NavPress products.

NAVPRESS
BRINGING TRUTH TO LIFE
www.navpress.com

Prices subject to change.